Casebook

for

Foundations of Financial Management

Fourteenth Edition

Stanley B. Block
Texas Christian University

Geoffrey A. Hirt
DePaul University

Bartley R. Danielsen
North Carolina State University

McGraw-Hill
Irwin

Casebook for
FOUNDATIONS OF FINANCIAL MANAGEMENT
Stanley B. Block, Geoffrey A. Hirt, and Bartley R. Danielsen

Published by McGraw-Hill/Irwin, an imprint of The McGraw-Hill Companies, Inc., 1221 Avenue of the Americas, New York, NY 10020.

1 2 3 4 5 6 7 8 9 0 WDQ/WDQ 1 0 9 8 7 6 5 4 3 2 1 0

ISBN: 978-0-07-731617-4
MHID: 0-07-731617-7

www.mhhe.com

Preface

This casebook is specifically designed for Block, Hirt, and Danielsen, *Foundations of Financial Management,* 13th edition. In a first course in finance, cases are only valuable if they tie in directly with the textual material, and that is precisely what this casebook is intended to do. In courses in advanced financial management, cases that relate to multiple textbooks are appropriate, but are of little value to the beginning student because of differences in terminology, methodological approaches, and so on.

The cases in this book fall somewhere between advanced problems and full-scale Harvard style cases. The authors have attempted to make the material both interesting and challenging. Many of the cases contain lively dialogue between the parties and topics such as surfing equipment, baseball cards, "Pac Man" merger defenses, and even Colonel Sanders and his Kentucky Fried Chicken restaurants. The end-of-case questions force the student to do multistep analysis and consider subjective issues as well. While many of the cases are hypothetical, they often contain comparative data on real world companies (such as Wal-Mart or JNB Realty Trust).

Material in the Table of Contents specifies the relationship of the case to the text. More specific information along these lines is also presented in the instructor's manual. The latter source also indicates the complexity of the case.

Two new cases have been added to this edition for a total of 33. While the total number of cases is relatively small, this book is specifically intended to service the 14th edition of Block, Hirt, and Danielsen and can provide interesting supplemental material for the instructor. It is not targeted for an actual case course.

The authors are indebted to Joe Andrew for his work in helping them develop some of the cases. We also thank professors Robert Fitzpatrick, Henry Kuniansky, and William Marsh for their contributions in case development. The users of this book should be aware that the authors were primarily involved in its development.

Stanley B. Block
Geoffrey A. Hirt
Bartley R. Danielsen

Contents

Case

1   **Harrod's Sporting Goods**   *Ratio Analysis* 1

2   **Chem-Med Company**   *Ratio Analysis* 5

3   **Glen Mount Furniture Company**   *Financial Leverage* 11

4   **Genuine Motor Products**   *Combined Leverage* 15

5   **Gale Force Surfing**   *Working Capital—Level vs. Seasonal Production* 21

6   **Modern Kitchenware Co.**   *Cash Discount* 25

7   **Landis Apparel Co.**   *Current Asset Management* 29

8   **Fresh & Fruity Foods, Inc.**   *Current Asset Management* 31

9   **Pierce Control Systems**   *Bank Financing* 35

10   **Allison Boone, M.D.**   *Time Value of Money* 39

11   **Billy Wilson, All American**   *Time Value of Money* 43

12   **Gilbert Enterprises**   *Stock Valuation* 47

13   **Baines Investments, Inc.**   *Stock Valuation* 51

14   **Altantic Airlines**   *Bond Valuation* 55

15   **Berkshire Instruments**   *Cost of Capital* 57

16   **Galaxy Systems, Inc.**   *Divisional Cost of Capital* 61

17   **Aerocomp, Inc.**   *Methods of Investment Evaluation* 65

18   **Phelps Toy Company**   *Capital Budgeting and Cash Flow* 69

19   **Global Resources**   *Risk-Adjusted Discount Rates* 73

20   **Inca, Inc.**   *Capital Budgeting with Risk* 77

21   **Robert Boyle & Associates, Inc.**   *Going Public and Investment Banking* 81

22   **Glazer Drug Company**   *Going Public* 87

23   **Leland Industries**   *Debt Financing* 89

24   **Warner Motor Oil Company**   *Bond Refunding* 93

25   **Midsouth Exploration Company**   *Preferred Stock* 95

26   **Alpha Biogenetics**   *Poison Pill* 99

27   **Montgomery Corporation**   *Dividend Policy* 103

28   **Orbit Chemical Company**   *Dividend Policy* 109

29   **Hamilton Products**   *Convertibles* 115

30   **Acme Alarm Systems**   *Merger Terms and Stock Price* 119

31   **Security Software, Inc.**   *Convertibles* 123

32   **National Brands vs. A-1 Holdings**   *Merger Analysis* 129

33   **KFC and the Colonel**   *General Business Consideration* 133

Harrod's Sporting Goods

Jim Harrod knew that service, above all, was important to his customers. Jim and Becky Harrod had opened their first store in Omaha, Nebraska in 1991. Harrod's carried a full line of sporting goods including everything from baseball bats and uniforms to fishing gear and hunting equipment. By the year 2009, there were twelve Harrod stores producing $5 million in total sales and generating a profit of over $200,000 per year.

On the positive side, there was an increasing demand for sporting goods as leisure time activities continued to grow. Also, the state of Nebraska, where all twelve stores were located, was experiencing moderate growth. Finally, there had been a sharp upturn in the last decade for women's sporting goods equipment. This was particularly true of softball uniforms for high school, college, and city league women's teams. Jim's wife Becky was one of the top softball players in the city of Omaha and her extensive contacts throughout the state help to bring in new business. While state, Omaha actually hosts the college baseball

Nebraska is primarily known as a football world series each year in June and this generates a lot of interest in baseball (and softball as well).

Jim, who had been a walk-on third string offensive tackle at the University of Nebraska (the Cornhuskers in Lincoln, Nebraska), took great pride in his stores as well as his prior university affiliation. He and Becky (also a University of Nebraska graduate in the mid-1980s) contributed $2,000 annually to the University of Nebraska athletic program.

The growth in the stores was the good news for Jim and Becky. The less than good news was the intense competition that they faced. Not only were they forced to compete with nationally established sporting good stores such as Oshman's and the Academy, but Wal-Mart also represented intense competition for the sporting goods dollar. The national stores were extremely competitive in terms of pricing. However, Jim, Becky and their employees offered great personal service, and they hoped this would allow them to continue with their specialty niche.

In January of 2010, Becky, who served as the company's chief financial officer, walked into Jim's office and said, "I've had it with the First National Bank of Omaha. It is willing to renew our loan and line of credit, but the bank wants to charge us 2½ percentage points over prime. The prime rate is the rate at which banks make loans to their most creditworthy customers. It was 4.75 percent at the time Becky had visited the bank, so that the total rate on the loan would be 7.25 percent. It was not so much the total rate that Becky objected to, as the fact that Harrod's was being asked to pay 2½ percent over prime. She felt that Harrod's was a strong enough company that one percent over prime should be all that the bank required. Her banker told her he would review the firm's financial statements with her next week and reconsider the premium Harrod's was being asked to pay over prime.

While Becky knew the bank "crunched all the numbers," she decided to do some additional financial analysis on her own. She had a bachelor's degree in finance with a 3.3 GPA. She began by examining Figures 1, 2, and 3.

Required

1. Compute the profitability ratios, including the a and b components (DuPont Methods) of ratios 2 and 3 as shown in the textbook. The profitability ratios should be shown for all three years.
2. Write a brief one-paragraph description of any trends that appear to have taken place over the three-year time period.
3. In examining the income statement in Figure 1, note that there was an extraordinary loss of $170,000 in 2009. This might have represented uninsured losses from a fire, a lawsuit settlement, etc. It probably does not represent a recurring event or affect the earnings capability of the firm. For that reason, the astute financial analyst might add back in the extraordinary loss to gauge the true operating earnings of the firm. Since it was a tax-deductible item, we must first multiply by (1-tax rate) before adding it back in.* The tax rate was 35 percent for the year.*

$170,000	Extraordinary loss
.65	(1-tax rate)
$110,500	Aftertax addition to profits from eliminating the extraordinary loss from net income

The more representative net income number for 2009 would now be:

Initially reported (Figure 1)	$200,318
Adjustment for extraordinary loss being eliminated	+110,500
Adjusted net income	$310,818

---

* This adjustment was made because the $170,000 deduction saved 35 percent of this amount in taxes. If we eliminate the $170,000, the tax benefit would also be eliminated. Thus, the firm would only benefit by 65 percent of $170,000, based on a 35 percent tax rate. The aftertax benefit of the tax adjustment for the extraordinary loss is $110,500.

Required

Based on the adjusted net income figure of $310,818, recompute the profitability ratios for 2009 (include part a and b for ratios 2 and 3).

4. Now with the adjusted net income numbers as part of the ratios for 2009, write a brief one-paragraph description of trends that appear to have taken place over the three-year time period (refer back to the data in Question 1 for 2007 and 2008).

5. Once again, using the revised profitability ratios for 2009 that you developed in Question 3, write a complete one paragraph analysis of the company's profitability ratios compared to the industry ratios (figure 3). Make sure to include asset turnover and debt to total assets as supplemental material in your analysis.

6. Harrod's has a superior sales to total assets ratio compared to the industry. For 2009, compute ratios 4, 6 and 7 as described in the text and compare them to industry data to see why this is so. Write a brief one-paragraph description of the results. Note: for ratio 4, only half the sales are on credit terms.

7. Conclusion: Based on your analysis in answering Questions 4 and 5, do you think that Becky Harrod has a legitimate complaint about being charged 2½ percent over prime instead of one percent over prime? There is no absolute right answer to this question, but use your best judgment.

Figure 1

Harrod's Sporting Goods

Income Statement
(2007-2009)

	2007	2008	2009
Sales	$4,269,871	$4,483,360	$5,021,643
Cost of goods sold	2,991,821	2,981,434	3,242,120
Gross Profit	1,278,050	1,501,926	1,779,523
Selling and administrative expense	865,450	1,004,846	1,175,100
Operating profit	412,600	497,080	604,423
Interest expense	115,300	122,680	126,241
Extraordinary loss	—	—	170,000
Net income before taxes	297,300	374,400	308,182
Taxes	104,100	131,300	107,864
Net income	$ 193,200	$ 243,100	$ 200,318

Figure 2

Harrod's Sporting Goods

Balance Sheet
(2007-2009)

	2007	2008	2009
Cash	$ 121,328	$ 125,789	$ 99,670
Marketable securities	56,142	66,231	144,090
Accounts receivable	341,525	216,240	398,200
Inventory	972,456	1,250,110	1,057,008
Total current assets	1,491,451	1,658,370	1,698,968
Net plant and equipment	1,678,749	1,702,280	1,811,142
Total assets	$3,170,200	$3,360,650	$3,510,110
Liabilities and Stockholders' Equity			
Accounts payable	$ 539,788	$ 576,910	$ 601,000
Notes payable	160,540	180,090	203,070
Total current liabilities	700,328	757,000	804,070
Long-term liabilities	1,265,272	1,292,995	1,372,240
Total liabilities	1,965,600	2,049,995	2,176,310
Common stock	367,400	368,000	368,000
Retained earnings*	837,200	942,665	965,800
Total Stockholders' equity	1,204,600	1,310,655	1,333,800
Total liabilities and stockholders' equity	$3,170,200	$3,360,650	$3,510,110

Figure 3

Harrod's Sporting Goods
Selected Industry Ratios for 2009

1.	Net income/Sales	4.51%
2a.	Net income/Total Assets	5.10%
2b.	Sales/Total Assets	1.33 x
3a.	Net income/Stockholder's Equity	9.80%
3b.	Debt/Total Assets	0.48
4.	Sales/Receivables	5.75 x
5.	Sales/Inventory	3.01 x
6.	Sales/Fixed Assets	3.20 x

---

* Withdrawal of funds in the form of dividends or other means makes the increase in retained earnings less than net income.

Chem-Med Company

April 9, 2008: Dr. Nathan Swan, age 40, chairman of the board of directors, chief executive officer, and founder of the Chem-Med Company, sat back in his chair and wondered if he wouldn't have been better off staying in his old job of teaching biochemistry at Harvard University. This business, he thought, was getting to be a headache. Just a short time ago, it seemed, he was able to spend most of his time in the company's lab comfortably working with test tubes and formulas. Lately, though, all his waking hours (or so it seemed) were taken up with columns of figures, dollars, and spreadsheets. It was true that he wanted the company to make money and grow; but he had no idea that the financial end of the business, about which he knew so little, would take up so much of his time.

Dr. Swan was a little mystified by financial matters. How did one describe a company in financial terms anyway? How did one tell if the company was in good or bad shape? (The amount of cash in the company's checking account didn't seem to be a sufficient indicator.) What on earth would one use to convince a bunch of hard-nosed investors that the company was capable of making a lot of money in the next few years if it just had some more money now? (Dr. Swan was always puzzled by the fact that Chem-Med was growing and making money, but it never seemed to have enough cash.)

Dr. Swan reflected back over Chem-Med's origins and the events that led up to today. Chem-Med began operations in 1997 after Dr. Swan completed the development of commercial-scale isolation of sodium hyaluronate (hereafter referred to as HA), a naturally occurring biological fluid that is useful in eye surgery and other medical and veterinary uses. The isolation process, complex and proprietary to the company, involves extracting and purifying HA from rooster combs. Initial seed money for the enterprise came from research grants from Harvard University and the U.S. Department of Agriculture (Food and Drug Admin-istration), plus contributions from Dr. Swan's colleague and associates, who were now classified as the company's stock-holders (254 as of April 2008, all closely held—not traded publicly).

In mid-2004, Chem-Med commenced the manufacture and distribution of its first product, VISCAM, which is used to hold tissues in place during and after surgery of the retina. In late 2005, Chem-Med received regulatory approval to market another HA product known as VISCHY, which is used for the treatment of degenerative joint diseases in horses. The two products, VISCHAM and VISCHY, are the only ones Chem-Med currently produces; however, the company has an active R&D program that is currently investigating other applications.

There are only two other manufacturers of FDA-approved HA products in the world: AB Fortia, a Swedish corporation, which manufactures a product called Healon in Sweden and distributes it in the United States through a subsidiary, Pharmacia, Inc.; and Cilco, Inc., of Huntington, West Virginia. Chem-Med has about a 25 percent share of the market (for HA products in eye surgery) against Cilco's 16 percent and Pharmacia's 59 percent. Pharmacia, with the power of giant AB Fortia behind it, waged a continuing marketing war with Chem-Med, undercutting Chem-Med's prices and wooing its costumers away at every opportunity. The matter came to a head in September, when Chem-Med filed a $13 million suit against Pharmacia, charging unfair trade practices. Dr. Swan was reasonably confident that Chem-Med would prevail in the suit, and, in fact, Pharmacia had recently offered to settle out of court for $500,000.

Dr. Swan's primary problem, he said, was that, although he was convinced the company was sound and would grow, he wasn't sure how to communicate that to potential investors in the financial community in a way that would convince them. Just handing out past income statements and balance sheets that he received from the accountants didn't seem to be enough. Further, he wasn't even sure the company needed outside financing, let alone how much. He just felt that they would need it, since they had always had to ask for money in the past.

Figure 1

CHEM-MED COMPANY
Income Statements

	2005—2007 (in 000s)			Pro Forma Income Statements		
	2005	*2006*	*2007*	*2008*	*2009*	*2010*
Net sales (all credit)	$ 777	$3,051	$3,814	$5,340	$7,475	$10,466
Cost of goods sold	257	995	1,040	1,716	2,154	3,054
Gross profit	520	2,056	2,774	3,624	5,321	7,412
Selling, etc., expenses	610	705	964	1,520	2,120	2,645
Other inc (exps)*	0	0	0	500	0	0
Operating profit	(90)	1,351	1,810	2,604	3,201	4,767
Interest expense	11	75	94	202	302	434
Income before tax	(101)	1,276	1,716	2,402	2,899	4,333
Income taxes (40% in 1986; 33% thereafter)	0	510	566	793	957	1,430
Net income	($ 101)	$ 766	$1,150	$1,609	$1,943	$ 2,903
Dividends paid	0	0	0	0	0	0
Increase in retained earnings	($ 101)	$ 766	$1,150	$1,609	$1,943	$ 2,903
Average number of shares**	2,326	2,326	2,347	2,347	2,347	2,347
Earnings per share	($ 0.04)	$ 0.33	$ 0.49	$ 0.69	$ 0.83	$ 1.24

* Other Inc (Exps) refers to extraordinary gains and losses. In 2008, $500,000 is expected from Pharmacia, Inc., in settlement of their suit.
** Shares are not publicly traded.

Figure 2

CHEM-MED COMPANY
Balance Sheets

	As of Dec. 31, years ended:			Pro Forma Balance Sheets As of Dec. 31, years ended:		
	2005	*2006*	*2007*	*2008*	*2009*	*2010*
Assets:						
Cash and equivalents	$ 124	$ 103	$ 167	$ 205	$ 422	$ 101
Accounts receivable	100	409	564	907	1,495	2,351
Inventories	151	302	960	1,102	1,443	798
Other current	28	59	29	41	57	11
Total current assets	403	873	1,720	2,255	3,417	3,261
Property, plant, and equipment	1,901	2,298	2,917	4,301	5,531	8,923
Less: accumulated depreciation	81	82	346	413	522	588
Property, plant, and equipment, net	1,820	2,216	2,571	3,888	5,009	8,335
Other fixed assets	0	101	200	200	215	399
Total assets	$2,223	$3,190	$4,491	$6,343	$8,641	$11,995
Liabilities:						
Accounts payable	210	$ 405	$ 551	$ 771	$1,080	$ 1,512
Short-term debt	35	39	42	59	82	135
Total current liabilities	245	444	593	830	1,162	1,647
Long-term debt	17	19	21	27	50	17
Total liabilities	262	463	614	857	1,212	1,664
Equity:						
Common stock	2,062	2,062	2,062	2,062	2,062	2,062
Retained earnings	(101)	665	1,815	3,424	5,366	8,269
Total equity	1,961	2,727	3,877	5,486	7,428	10,331
Total liabilities and equity	$2,223	$3,190	$4,491	$ 6,343	$8,641	$11,995

Dr. Swan had lunch with his banker just recently, and the banker mentioned several restrictive covenants that the company would have to meet if it came to the bank for financing. Dr. Swan pulled a sheet of paper from his desk drawer and glanced at it. There were three covenants listed:

- The current ratio must be maintained above 2.25 to 1.
- The debt-to-assets ratio must be less than .3 to 1.
- Dividends cannot be paid unless earnings are positive.

Dr. Swan didn't think he would have any trouble with those, but he wasn't sure. Then he suddenly remembered he was supposed to meet a representative from one of the local supermarket chains (who supplied Chem-Med with rooster combs) in five minutes. He hurriedly put his papers away and wished he had more time to analyze the numbers before the next board of directors meeting. (The financial information is presented in Figures 1, 2, and 3.)

Figure 3

Biotechnology Industry Statistics
Median Company in SIC 2831
Biological Products*

	2005	2006	2007
Current ratio	2.5	2.3	2.4
Quick ratio	1.2	1.1	1.3
Inventory turnover	5.5	5.6	5.7
Total asset turnover	1.15	1.16	1.18
Return on sales	4.00%	4.00%	5.00%
Return on assets	4.60%	4.64$	5.90%
Return on equity	7.64%	8.44%	12.29%
Total debt to assets	0.40	0.45	0.52

Selected Statistics
Pharmacia Company

	2005	2006	2007
Current ratio	2.8	2.7	2.8
Quick ratio	1.5	1.3	1.6
Inventory turnover	5.6	5.7	5.8
Total asset turnover	1.9	2	1.9
Return on sales	6.00%	6.50%	7.00%
Return on assets	11.40%	13.00%	13.30%
Return on equity	19.04%	27.66%	29.56%
Total debt to assets	0.40	0.53	0.55
Price-earnings ratio	13.7	14	15
Average stock price	$21.78	$24.92	$31.50

* Source: Dun's Industry Ratios. The data have been adjusted for this case.

Required

You are an investor who is considering adding Chem-Med to your portfolio. As such, you are interested in the company's record of profitability, prospects for the future, degree of risk, and how it compares with others in the industry. From that point of view, answer the following questions:

1. What was Chem-Med's rate of sales growth in 2007? What is it forecasted to be in 2008, 2009, and 2010?
2. What was Chem-Med's net income growth in 2007? What is it forecasted to be in 2008, 2009, and 2010? Is projected net income growing faster or slower than projected sales? After computing these values, take a hard look at the 2008 income statement data to see if you want to make any adjustments.
3. How does Chem-Med's current ratio for 2007 compare to Pharmacia's? How does it compare to the industry average? Compute Chem-Med's current ratio for 2010. Is there any problem with it?
4. What is Chem-Med's total debt-to-assets ratio for 2007, 2008, 2009, 2010? Is any trend evident in the four-year period? Does Chem-Med in 2007 have more or less debt than the average company in the industry?
5. What is Chem-Med's average accounts receivable collection period for 2007, 2008, 2009, 2010? Is the period getting longer or shorter? What are the consequences?
6. How does Chem-Med's return-on-equity ratio (ROE) compare to Pharmacia's and the industry for 2007? Using the Du Pont method, compare the positions of Chem-Med and Pharmacia. Compute ROE for each company using the following formula:

    ROE = Profit margin x Asset turnover/(1—Debt to assets)

    Compare the results to determine the sources of ROE for each company.

Glen Mount Furniture Company

Furniture magnate Carl Thompson couldn't believe the amount of pressure security analysts could put on a firm. The Glen Mount Furniture Company was a leading manufacturer of fine home furnishings and distributed its product directly to department stores, independent home furnishing retailers, and a few regional furniture chains. The firm specialized in bedroom, dining room, and living room furniture and had three plants in North Carolina and two in Virginia. Its home office was in High Point, North Carolina.

In a recent presentation to the Atlanta chapter of the Financial Analysts Federation, Carl Thompson barely had taken a bite out of his salad when two analysts from Smith Barney, Harris Upham & Co., a stock brokerage firm, began asking questions. They were particularly concerned about Glen Mount's growth rate in earnings per share.

Carl was aware that security analysts considered earnings performance to be important, but he was somewhat distressed by the fact that this seemed to be their overriding concern. It bothered him that the firm had just spent over $10 million to develop exciting new product lines, modernize production facilities, and expand distribution capabilities, and yet all the questions seemed to deal with near term earnings performance. He felt that he would eventually have an opportunity to discuss the above-mentioned management initiatives and their impact on the company for the next decade, but current earnings per share seemed to gather the attention of the analysts.

Carl knew only too well from past experience that the earnings performance of the firm would affect the company's price-earnings ratio and its market value. Furthermore, before Carl became president of Glen Mount Furniture Company, he had attended a six-week Executive Development Program at the Harvard Business School in which he heard a number of professors stress the importance of the goal of stockholder wealth maximization. He often wondered if other items were not equally important to the company, such as community service (the firm donated $60,000 a year to a local university to help supplement faculty salaries for outstanding professors). He also had a sense of pride that his firm provided employment to over 500 people in the area. He was not sure that the security analysts would consider these items to be of particular importance.

With all of these thoughts in mind, his upcoming meeting with Chief Financial Officer Barbara Bainesworth became particularly important.

When Barbara arrived, she had a number of financial documents to review for the purpose of making key decisions. In Figure 1, she showed the earnings performance of the company over the last five years. Figure 2 provided a current balance sheet, and Figure 3 represented an abbreviated income statement for 2010.

The firm was considering buying back 625,000 shares of stock outstanding at $16 per share. This would represent $10 million in total. The funds to purchase the shares would be acquired from a new bond issue that would carry an interest rate of 11.25 percent. The bond would have a 15-year life. The firm was in a 34 percent tax bracket.

Figure 1   Earnings per share for the last five years

Year	1st Quarter	2nd Quarter	3rd Quarter	4th Quarter	Yearly Total
2003	$.23	$.25	$.19	$.34	$1.01
2004	.26	.28	.27	.41	1.22
2005	.34	.36	.33	.48	1.51
2006	.35	.37	.34	.49	1.55
2007	.35	.36	.36	.49	1.56

Figure 2

GLEN MOUNT FURNITURE COMPANY

Balance Sheet

December 31, 2010

Assets

Current assets:		
Cash		$ 350,000
Marketable securities		90,000
Accounts receivable		5,000,000
Inventory		7,000,000
Total current assets		12,440,000
Other Assets:		
Investments		5,000,000
Fixed Assets		
Plant and equipment	27,060,000	
Less: Accumulated depreciation	4,000,000	
Net plant and equipment		23,060,000
Total assets		$ 40,500,000

Liabilities and Stockholders' Equity

Current liabilities:	
Accounts payable	$ 4,400,000
Wages payable	150,000
Accrued expenses	950,000
Total current liabilities	5,500,000
Long-term liabilities	
Bonds payable, 10.625%	12,000,000
Stockholders' equity	
Common stock, $1 par value, 2,000,000 shares	2,000,000
Capital in excess of par	8,000,000
Retained earnings	13,000,000
Total stockholders' equity	23,000,000
Total liabilities and stockholders' equity	40,500,000

Figure 3

GLEN MOUNT FURNITURE COMPANY

Abbreviated Income Statement

For the Year Ended December 31, 2010

Sales	$45,000,000
Less: Fixed Costs	12,900,000
Less: Variable Costs (58% of sales)	26,100,000
Operating income (EBIT)	$ 6,000,000
Less: Interest	1,275,000
Earnings before taxes (EBT)	$ 4,725,000
Less: Taxes (34%)	1,606,500
Earnings after taxes (EAT)	$ 3,118,500
Shares	2,000,000
Earnings per share	$ 1.56

Required

1. Project earnings per share for 2011 assuming that sales increase by $500,000. Use Figure 3 as the model for the calculation. Further assume that the capital structure is not changed.
2. By what percent did earnings per share increase from 2010 to 2011?
3. Now assume that $10 million of debt replaces 625,000 shares of common stock as described in the case. The interest on the new debt will be 11.25 percent. What will projected earnings per share be for 2011 based on the anticipated sales increase of $500,000?
4. Based on your answer to question 3, by what percent would earnings per share increase from 2010 to 2011?
5. Compute the degree of financial leverage (DFL) for the answer to question 1 and for the answer to question 3.
6. Using the formula in footnote 3 of Chapter 5, compute degree of combined leverage (DCL) for the answer to question 1 and the answer to question 3.
7. What is the total debt to assets ratio as shown in the 2010 balance sheet (Figure 2)? What will it be if $10 million worth of stockholders' equity is replaced with debt?
8. What do you think might happen to the stock price as a result of replacing $10 million worth of stockholders' equity with debt? Consider any relevant factors.

4

Genuine Motor Products

Genuine Motor Products, located in Northern Ohio, manufactures precision measuring devices to monitor exhaust emission systems for new and used automobiles. Its products are sold worldwide.

The firm hired Mike Anton in January of 2009 as vice president in charge of manufacturing operations. Mike had a bachelor's degree in industrial engineering from Case Western Reserve University and an MBA from Ohio State University. He had spent the last 15 years working for General Motors (Arlington, Texas division), Toyota Motor Corp., and Volvo. At age 38, he had established a good reputation for innovation within the auto and auto parts industry.

Upon being hired, he began looking over the financial statements, particularly the balance sheet as of December 31, 2008 and the pro forma income statement for 2009 as shown in Figure 1 and 2, respectively. His immediate reaction was that the firm had not made the move to automation that others in the industry had. The company's manufacturing process was highly labor intensive as indicated by the fact that fixed assets (net plant and equipment) represented only $8 million out of total assets of $24 million (Figure 1) and that variable costs per unit were $25 in comparison to a sales price of $30 per unit (Figure 2).

Although he thought the pro forma income statement for 2009 as shown in Figure 2 looked reasonably good, he believed returns could be better if the firm went to greater automation and was less dependent on labor and expensive materials.

When he shared his thoughts with Harry Engle, the chief financial officer, the response he received was lukewarm. Harry had been with the firm in good times as well as bad over the last 20 years and was quick to point out the advantages of not being tied up with a lot of fixed costs and debt during a slowdown in sales in the auto industry. As Harry was fond of saying, "Genuine Motor Products does not have a labor union and when business is bad, we lay people off. By gosh, you can't lay machinery and equipment off."

Figure 1

GENUINE MOTOR PRODUCTS

Balance Sheet

As of December 31, 2008

Assets

Current assets..		$16,000,000
Fixed assets		
Plant and equipment	$20,000,000	
Less: accumulated depreciation..	12,000,000	
Net plant and equipment..		8,000,000
Total assets		$24,000,000

Liabilities and Stockholders' Equity

Current liabilities..		10,000,000
Long-term liabilities:		
Bonds payable 10.75%		2,000,000
Total liabilities..		$12,000,000
Stockholders' equity:		
Common stock, $1 par value, 2,000,000 shares		$ 2,000,000
Capital in excess of par...		4,000,000
Retained earnings		6,000,000
Total stockholders' equity		$12,000,000
Total liabilities and stockholders' equity....................................		$24,000,000

Figure 2

GENUINE MOTOR PRODUCTS

Pro forma Income Statement

For 2009

Sales (1,000,000 units @ $30 per unit)	$30,000,000
– Fixed costs*	2,000,000
– Total variable costs (1,000,000 units @ $25 per unit	25,000,000
Operating income (EBIT)..	$ 3,000,000
– Interest (10.75% x $2,000,000)	215,000
Earnings before taxes	$ 2,785,000
– Taxes (35%)	974,750
Earnings after taxes	$ 1,810,250
Shares	2,000,000
Earnings per share	$ .91

* Fixed costs include$1,000,000 in depreciation

In spite of Harry's arguments, Mike Anton was determined to show the impact of both operating and financial leverage on Genuine Motor Products operations. He reconstructed the year-end balance sheet for 2008 (previously shown in Figure 1), and the results are shown in Figure 3 based on the following assumptions.

1. That the firm would increase fixed assets by $14 million dollars.
2. That $10 million of the $14 would be funded through long-term debt in the form of additional bonds payable at an interest rate of 10.75%.
3. The remaining $4 million would come from the sale of additional common stock at a net price to the corporation of $12.50. This would require the issuance of 320,000 new shares ($4 million/$12.50 = 320,000 shares).

The impact of these values on the balance sheet in Figure 3 shows substantially greater leverage both on the asset and liability side.

Figure 3

GENUINE MOTOR PRODUCTS

Revised Balance Sheet

For the year ended December 31, 2008

Assets

Current assets		$16,000,000
Fixed Assets		
Plant and equipment	$34,000,000	
Less: Accumulated depreciation	12,000,000	
Net plant and equipment		22,000,000
Total assets		$38,000,000

Liabilities and Stockholders' Equity

Current liabilities	10,000,000
Long-term liabilities:	
Bonds payable 10.75%	12,000,000
Total liabilities	$22,000,000
Stockholders' equity:	
Common stock, $1 par value, 2,320,000 shares	$ 2,320,000*
Capital in excess of par	7,680,000**
Retained earnings	6,000,000
Total stockholders' equity	$16,000,000
Total liabilities and stockholders' equity	$38,000,000

*2,000,000 old shares + 320,000 new shares = 2,320,000 shares

** 4,000,000 old capital in excess of par + 320,000 new shares x ($12.50 price – $1 par value) =
4,000,000 + 320,000 ($11.50) = $7,680,000

The intent of using more leverage was to increase the potential profitability of the firm. You are called in as a financial analyst to rework the 2009 pro forma income statement based on the assumptions stated in Table 1. These primarily relate to the fact there are now more fixed assets, long-term debt, and shares outstanding.

Table 1
Assumptions for Revised Pro Forma Income Statement

1. Sales will remain constant at 1,000,000 units at $30 per unit.
2. Fixed costs will increase from $2,000,0000 to $5,800,000, a gain of $3,800,000. (Depreciation expense will be $2,800,000 and this will be shown as a footnote in the 2009 pro forma income statement).
3. Variable cost per unit will be reduced from $25 to $18.80. A total of 1,000,000 units will still be sold. The reduction in variable costs per unit is a direct result of the increased fixed costs and the associated automation.
4. Interest expense will reflect that there is now $12 million in long-term debt in the form of bonds payable at 10.75%. Ten million dollars of new debt is being added to $2 million of old debt.
5. Shares outstanding are now at a level of 2,320,000. Three hundred and twenty thousand new shares are being added to the 2,000,000 old shares currently outstanding.

Required

1. Complete the revised pro forma income statement below. In the process, refer back to Figure 2, the original pro forma income statement for 2009 and the assumptions in Table 1. The new statement you are developing below will be referred to as Figure 4 for purposes of reference.

Figure 4

GENUINE MOTOR PRODUCTS
Revised Pro forma Income Statement
For 2009

Sales (1,000,000 units @ $30 per unit)	$30,000,000
– Fixed costs*	5,800,000
– Total variable costs (1,000,000 units @ $18.80 per unit	
Operating income (EBIT)	
– Interest (10.75% x $12,000,000)	
Earnings before taxes	
– Taxes (35%)	
Earnings after taxes	
Shares	2,320,000
Earnings per share	$ 1.15

* Fixed costs include $2,800,000 in depreciation

Required

2. Explain the primary reasons for the change in earnings per share between Figure 2 and Figure 4.

3. To determine the extent the company is more leveraged than it was prior to changes suggested by Mike Anton, compute degree of operating leverage (DOL), degree of financial leverage (DFL), and degree of combined leverage (DCL) both for Figure 2 (before changes) and Figure 4 (after changes). Use equations 5–3, 5–5, and 5–7 from the text.

4. Using the same financial statements (Figure 2 and Figure 4), compute the breakeven point before and after the changes. Use equation 5–1 from the text.

5. Assume you use a different measure of break-even analysis. The answer to question 4 tells you the number of units the firm needs to sell to cover fixed costs. Assume you are interested in covering all cash outflows and, furthermore, will use only cash flow numbers rather than accounting numbers. The cash outflows to be covered are (Fixed costs – depreciation) plus interest payments.

   The formula for the revised break-even (BE) point is:

   $$\text{Revised BE} = \frac{(\text{Fixed costs - depreciation}) + \text{Interest}}{\text{Price}\,(\text{P}) - (\text{VC})\,\text{variable cost per unit}}$$

   Apply this formula to Figure 2 to get the revised break-even point before the changes and Figure 4 to get the revised break-even point after the changes. (Note the value for depreciation can be found as a footnote at the bottom of the two figures).

6. Harry Engle suggests that the company could be in trouble if Mike Anton's changes are put in place (as reflected in Figure 4) and sales volume is only 300,000 units. Using your revised break-even answers from question 5, do you agree?

7. Finally, assume sales volume reaches 1,500,000 units after Mike Anton's changes are put into place. What will the new figure be for earnings per share? Under the old plan, earnings per share at 1,500,000 units would be $1.72.

Sales (1,500,000 units @ $30 per unit)..................................... $45,000,000
– Fixed costs 5,800,000
– Total variable costs (1,500,000 units @ $18.80 per unit)
Operating income...
– Interest (10.75% x $12,000,000)...
Earnings before taxes..
– Taxes (35%) ....
Earnings after taxes..
Shares.. 2,320,000
Earnings per share..

8. After computing all the numbers in the case, are you inclined to agree with Mike Anton that the changes to automation would be a good idea or Harry Engle, the chief financial officer, that they would not be? What is likely to be the key variable in determining the success or failure of the new plan?

CASE

5

Gale Force Surfing

During mid-September 2008, the top managers of the Gale Force Corporation, a leading manufacturer of windsurfing equipment and surfboards, were gathered in the president's conference room reviewing the results of the company's operations during the past fiscal year (which runs from October 1 to September 30).

"Not a bad year, on the whole," remarked the president, 32-year-old Charles ("Chuck") Jamison. "Sales were up, profits were up, and our return on equity was a respectable 15 percent. In fact," he continued, "the only dark spot I can find in our whole annual report is the profit margin, which is only 2.25 percent. Seems like we ought to be making more than that, don't you think, Tim?" He looked across the table at the vice president for finance, Timothy Baggit, age 28.

"I agree," replied Tim, "and I'm glad you brought it up, because I have a suggestion on how to improve that situation." He leaned forward in his chair as he realized he had captured the interest of the others. "The problem is, we have too many expenses on our income statement that are eating up the profits. Now, I've done some checking, and the expenses all seem to be legitimate except for interest expense. Look here, we paid over $250,000 last year to the bank just to finance our short-term borrowing. If we could have kept that money instead, our profit margin ratio would have been 4.01 percent, which is higher than any other firm in the industry."

"But, Tim, we have to borrow like that," responded Roy ("Pop") Thomas, age 35, the vice president for production. "After all, our sales are seasonal, with almost all occurring between March and September. Since we don't have much money coming in from October to February, we have to borrow to keep the production line going."

"Right," Tim replied, "and it's the production line that's the problem. We produce the same number of products every month, no matter what we expect sales to be. This causes inventory to build up when sales are slow and to deplete when sales pick up. That fluctuating inventory causes all sorts of problems, including the excessive amount of borrowing we have to do to finance the inventory accumulation." (See Tables 1 through 5 for details of Gale Force's current operations based on equal monthly production.)

Table 1   Sales Forecast (in units)

First Quarter		Second Quarter		Third Quarter		Fourth Quarter	
October 2007	150	January	0	April	500	July	1,000
November	75	February	0	May	1,000	August	500
December	25	March	300	June	1,000	September	250

Table 2   Production Schedule and Inventory (equal monthly production)

	Beginning Inventory		Production This Month		Sales		End Inventory	Inventory ($2,000 per unit)
October 2007	400	+	400	−	150	=	650	$1,300,000
November	650		400		75		975	1,950,000
December	975		400		25		1,350	2,700,000
January	1,350		400		0		1,750	3,500,000
February	1,750		400		0		2,150	4,300,000
March	2,150		400		300		2,250	4,500,000
April	2,250		400		500		2,150	4,300,000
May	2,150		400		1,000		1,550	3,100,000
June	1,550		400		1,000		950	1,900,000
July	950		400		1,000		350	700,000
August	350		400		500		250	500,000
September	250		400		250		400	800,000

Table 3   Sales Forecast, Cash Receipts and Payments, and Cash Budget

	October 2007	November	December	January	February	March
Sales Forecast						
Sales (units)	150	75	25	0	0	300
Sales (unit price: $3,000)	$ 450,000	$ 225,000	$ 75,000	0	0	$ 900,000
Cash Receipts Schedule						
50% cash	$ 225,000	$ 112,500	$ 37,500			$ 450,000
50% from prior month's sales*	$ 375,000	$ 225,000	$ 112,500	$ 37,500	0	0
Total cash receipts	$ 600,000	$ 337,500	$ 150,000	$ 37,500	0	$ 450,000
Cash Payments Schedule						
Production in units	400	400	400	400	400	400
Production costs (each = $2,000)	$ 800,000	$ 800,000	$ 800,000	$ 800,000	$ 800,000	$ 800,000
Overhead	$ 200,000	$ 200,000	$ 200,000	$ 200,000	$ 200,000	$ 200,000
Dividends and interest	0	0	0	0	0	0
Taxes	$ 150,000	0	0	$ 150,000	0	0
Total cash payments	$ 1,150,000	$ 1,000,000	$ 1,000,000	$ 1,150,000	$ 1,000,000	$ 1,000,000
Cash Budget; Required Minimum Balance is $125,000						
Cash flow	$ −550,000	−662,500	−850,000	−1,112,500	−1,000,000	−550,000
Beginning cash	125,000	125,000	125,000	125,000	125,000	125,000
Cumulative cash balance	−425,000	−537,500	−725,000	−987,500	−875,000	−425,000
Monthly loan or (repayment)	$ 550,000	$ 662,500	$ 850,000	$ 1,112,500	$ 1,000,000	$ 550,000
Cumulative loan	$ 550,000	$ 1,212,500	$ 2,062,500	$ 3,175,000	$ 4,175,000	$ 4,725,000
Ending cash balance	$ 125,000	$ 125,000	$ 125,000	$ 125,000	$ 125,000	$ 125,000

*September sales assumed to be $750,000.

"Now, here's my idea," said Tim. "Instead of producing 400 items a month, every month, we match the production schedule with the sales forecast. For example, if we expect to sell 150 windsurfers in October, then we only make 150. That way we avoid borrowing to make the 250 more that we don't expect to sell, anyway. Over the course of an entire year the savings in interest expense could really add up."

"Hold on, now," Pop responded, feeling that his territory was being threatened. "That kind of scheduling really fouls up things in the shop where it counts. It causes a feast or famine environment—nothing to do for one month, then a deluge the next. It's terrible for the employees, not to mention the supervisors who are trying to run an efficient operation. Your idea may make the income statements look good for now, but the whole company will suffer in the long run."

Chuck intervened. "OK, you guys, calm down. Tim may have a good idea or he may not, but at least it's worth looking into. I propose that you all work up two sets of figures, one assuming level production and one matching production with sales. We'll look at them both and see if Tim's idea really does produce better results. If it does, we'll check it further against other issues Pop is concerned about and then make a decision on which alternative is better for the firm."

Table 3 *(continued)*

	April	May	June	July	August	September
Sales Forecast						
Sales (units).....................................	500	1,000	1,000	1,000	500	250
Sales (unit price: $3,000)................	$1,500,000	$3,000,000	$3,000,000	$3,000,000	$1,500,000	$ 750,000
Cash Receipts Schedule						
50% cash	$ 750,000	$1,500,000	$1,500,000	$1,500,000	$ 750,000	$ 375,000
50% from prior month's sales.........	$ 450,000	$ 750,000	$1,500,000	$1,500,000	$1,500,000	$ 750,000
Total cash receipts	$1,200,000	$2,250,000	$3,000,000	$3,000,000	$2,250,000	$ 1,125,000
Cash Payments Schedule						
Production in units..........................	400	400	400	400	400	400
Production costs (each = $2,000) ...	$ 800,000	$ 800,000	$ 800,000	$ 800,000	$ 800,000	$ 800,000
Overhead.......................................	$ 200,000	$ 200,000	$ 200,000	$ 200,000	$ 200,000	$ 200,000
Dividends and interest	0	0	0	0	$1,000,000	0
Taxes	$ 150,000	0	0	$ 300,000	0	0
Total cash payments.................	$1,150,000	$1,000,000	$1,000,000	$1,300,000	$2,000,000	$1,000,000
Cash Budget; Required Minimum Balance is $125,000						
Cash flow	50,000	1,250,000	2,000,000	1,700,000	250,000	125,000
Beginning cash...............................	125,000	125,000	125,000	125,000	400,000	650,000
Cumulative cash balance	175,000	1,375,000	2,125,000	1,825,000	650,000	775,000
Monthly loan or (repayment)	($ 50,000)	($1,250,000)	($2,000,000)	($1,425,000)	0	0
Cumulative loan.............................	$4,675,000	$3,425,000	$1,425,000	0	0	0
Ending cash balance.......................	$ 125,000	$ 125,000	$ 125,000	$ 400,000	$ 650,000	$ 775,000

Table 4
Total Current Assets
First Year

	Cash		Accounts Receivable*		Inventory		Total Current Assets
October	$125,000	+	$225,000	+	$1,300,000	=	$1,650,000
November	125,000		112,500		1,950,000		2,187,500
December............	125,000		37,500		2,700,000		2,862,500
January................	125,000		0		3,500,000		3,625,000
February..............	125,000		0		4,300,000		4,425,000
March..................	125,000		450,000		4,500,000		5,075,000
April....................	125,000		750,000		4,300,000		5,175,000
May.....................	125,000		1,500,000		3,100,000		4,725,000
June.....................	125,000		1,500,000		1,900,000		3,525,000
July......................	400,000		1,500,000		700,000		2,600,000
August.................	650,000		750,000		500,000		1,900,000
September	775,000		375,000		800,000		1,950,000

* Equals 50 percent of monthly sales

Table 5   Cumulative loan balance and interest expense (1% per month)

	October	November	December	January	February	March
Cumulative loan balance	$ 550,000	$1,212,500	$2,062,500	$3,175,000	$4,175,000	$4,725,000
Interest expense at (prime, 8.0%, + 4.0%) 12.00%..............	$ 5,500	$ 12,125	$ 20,625	$ 31,750	$ 41,750	$ 47,250

	April	May	June	July	August	September
Cumulative loan balance	$4,675,000	$3,425,000	$1,425,000	0	0	0
Interest expense at (prime, 8.0%, + 4.0%) 12.00%..............	$ 46,750	$ 34,250	$ 14,250	0	0	0

Total interest expense for the year: $254,250

Required

1. Tables 1 through 5 contain the financial information describing the effects of level production on inventory, cash flow, loan balances, and interest expense. Reproduce these tables if Tim's suggestion were implemented; that is, change the *Production This Month* column in Table 2 from 400 each month to 150, 75, 25, and so on, to match *Sales* in the next column. Then recompute the remainder of Table 2, and Tables 3, 4, and 5 based on the new production numbers. Beginning inventory is still 400 units. Beginning cash is still $125,000 and that remains the minimum required balance.

2. Given that Gale Force is charged 12 percent annual interest (1 percent a month) on its cumulative loan balance each month (Table 5), how much would Tim's suggestion save in interest expense in a year?

3. Up until now, we have not considered any inefficiencies that have been introduced as a result of going from level to seasonal production. Assume that there is an added expense for each sales dollar of .5 percent (.005). Based on this fact and the information computed in question 2, is seasonal production justified?

Modern Kitchenware Co.

Modern Kitchenware Co. specializes in the manufacturing and distribution of items used in the kitchen. Among its many products are microwave ovens, toasters, electric can openers, etc. Its home base is in Kansas City and the firm sells to retailers throughout the U.S. and Canada. Its customers range from small retail outlets in strip shopping centers to major customers such as Sears and J. C. Penney. In the most recent fiscal year, its sales were $18 million with $2,500,000 in aftertax profits.

The firm's CEO is Beth Graham, who holds a B.A. in economics from St. Louis University. Beth has moved up through the ranks as both a product manager and VP of marketing.

She has implemented an inventory control system that was thought by many to be the finest in the kitchen supply industry. The computer-based system kept hourly tabs on inventory in stock at Kansas City as well as the ten distribution centers throughout the country.

Management of Accounts Receivable

Beth felt a good deal less confident about the firm's ability to control and manage the level of accounts receivable.

Historically, the firm shipped out its goods with a 30-day pay period allowed, with no cash discount offered. An analysis of current accounts receivable indicated the pattern of receivables shown in Table 1.

In looking over the numbers, Beth felt the customers, on average, were taking over 30 days to pay. The receivables were based on average daily credit sales of $54,274 throughout the year.

Beth called in Al Becker, the chief financial officer, and asked him what he thought the problem was. He said that because no cash discount was being offered for early payment, customers were sometimes lax in their payment pattern.

A Potential Cash Discount

Beth told Al to consider the impact of a cash discount on the accounts receivable balance of the firm as well as its profitability.

Following Beth's instructions, Al evaluated the effect of the three alternative cash discount policies shown in Table 2.

He ran some pilot studies among customers and determined the results below.

Ten percent of the customers would take advantage of the 1 percent discount by paying within 10 days. If the two percent discount were offered, 25 percent would take it, and if the 3 percent discount were offered, 60 percent of the customers would take advantage of it. In each case, it was assumed that those who do not take the discount would pay at the end of 30 days.

Table 1. Accounts Receivables Outstanding, December 2006

Days Outstanding		Amount
0 – 10 days		20,000
10 – 20 days		150,000
20 – 30 days		400,000
30 – 40 days		650,000
40 – 50 days		430,000
50 – 60 days		350,000
	Total A/R	2,000,000

Table 2. New Terms for Cash Discounts

Alternative	Terms
1	1/10, net 30
2	2/10, net 30
3	3/10, net 30

He then computed the new average collection period(s) based on the data in the prior paragraph. With an assumption of average daily credit sales remaining at $54,274 per day, he also computed the anticipated new accounts receivable balance based on the three different cash discount policies.

He was informed by his corporate treasurer that any freed up funds from accounts receivable could be used elsewhere in the corporation to earn a return of 18 percent.

All this information was reported back to Beth, and she suggested that a thorough analysis be conducted of all the implications of the cash discount policies.

Required

1. Compute the current average collection period based on the data in Table 1. In doing this, multiply the midpoint of the days outstanding, by the weight assigned to that category. For example, the midpoint of the second company is 15 days and the category represents 7.5 percent of total accounts receivable ($150,000/$2,000,000). Its value is 1.125 days (15 days x .075). After this process is followed for all six categories, add up the total to get the average collection period.

2. Compute the new average collection period based on the terms in Table 2 and the results of the pilot study. Use the simplifying assumption that under the new policies all customers will all pay at the end of the 10th day or the end of the 30th day.
   i.e., for the 1/10, net 30
   10% x 10 days = 1 day
   90% x 30 days = 27 days
                    28 days average collection period

3. Assuming average daily credit sales remain at $54,274 per day, what will be the new accounts receivable balance based on the three new cash discount policies?
   Accounts receivable = average collection period x average daily credit sales

4. Compute the cost of the cash discount based on the three policies under consideration. Recall that total credit sales were $18 million.
   Multiply total credit sales times the percent that use the discount for each new discount policy times the size of the discount.

5. Compute the amount of freed up funds based on the three different cash discount policies based on the following:
   Old accounts receivable (given in table 1)
   New accounts receivable (Question 3)
   Freed up funds

6. Assuming an 18 percent return can be earned on the freed up funds, what is the return that can be earned under the three cash discount policies?

7. Subtract the cost of the cash discount (Question 4) from the return on the freed up funds (Question 6) to determine the actual profitability or loss under the three cash discount policies.
   Which of the three policies is the most profitable?

8. After looking at all the data, Beth decides to only consider Alternatives 1 and 2. She decides that the 2/10, net 30 cash discount could increase credit sales by $1 million. The 1/10, net 30 is assumed to have no impact on sales. Assume a 9 percent before tax profit margin on the new sales.* Also assume the 2 percent cash discount must be subtracted. Further, assume the new sales will require a new investment in accounts receivable of $27,750. These funds could earn 20% if invested elsewhere. (The 20% is return on investment, whereas the 9% referred to above is return on sales.)

Required

Under the new set of facts, is the 2/10, net 30 policy now superior to the 1/10, net 30 policy?

Take the profitability computed for the 2/10, net 30 policy in Question 7, and add to that the increased profitability (9% return minus costs) detailed above. Compare your new total answers for the profitability of the 2/10, net 30 policy to the answer for the 1/10, net 30 policy in Question 7.

Which policy should the firm choose?

---

* You do not have to include taxes for any of the calculations in this case.

Landis Apparel Co.

Ruth Landis was carefully considering the firm's sales prospects for 2011. Her firm, located in Southern California, did slightly over $100 million in sales. She and her husband, Jim, started the women clothier's company two decades ago and has watched it grow from five employees to over 500. Ruth was the CEO and Jim was the chief financial officer. Landis produced its own brand of dresses, sweaters, and other apparel, and also sold brands licensed by Tommy Hilfiger, Givenchy, Espirit, and others. Landis' dress manufacturing plants were located in Southern California, South America, and Asia.

Among the many hundreds of decisions Ruth and Jim Landis had to make was what customers were acceptable for credit extension. In the retail fashion business, virtually no customer paid cash, so the extension of credit to retailers was critical in doing business.

A potential account has been brought to their attention by the credit department.

On routine decisions the credit department determined what accounts were acceptable, but on more involved situations the final call rested at the top with Ruth and Jim Landis.

The Potential Account

The account under consideration was Monique Fashion Stores. They were asking for $1 million for credit purchases. Based on Monique's Dun & Bradstreet rating and other industry data, there appeared to be a five percent probability of non-payment if credit were extended. The collection costs to service the account were four percent of sales and the production and selling costs were 85 percent of sales. Any profits would be taxed at a 35 percent rate. Ruth and Jim determined that accounts receivable turnover would be three times. The firm had a required return on investment of 14 percent.

Required

1. Using techniques similar to that under "An Actual Credit Decision" in Chapter 7 of the Block and Hirt text, determine the "Annual Incremental Income after Taxes," from making the sale to Monique Fashion Stores.

2. Assume the only new investment would be in accounts receivable. Based on the turnover ratio of three times, what would the investment in accounts receivable be?

3. Compute the return on accounts receivable based on your answers to questions one and two.

4. Given that the firm has a required return on investment of 14 percent, should Landis Apparel Co. sell to Monique Fashion Stores?

5. If the accounts receivable turnover ratio were four times and the other percentages were the same, should Landis Apparel Co. make the sale?

6. Now assume that $200,000 in inventory must be maintained throughout the year in addition to the accounts receivable balance you computed in question 5. Should Landis Apparel Co. make the sale?

7. Continue to assume the same facts in question 6, but with one other change. By manufacturing the merchandise overseas, Landis Apparel Co. can cut back production and selling costs to 75 percent of sales. Now recompute "Annual Incremental Income after Taxes." Then divide the number by the total investment found in question 6. Should Landis Apparel Co. make the sale?

8

Fresh & Fruity Foods, Inc.

Fresh & Fruity Foods is a mail-order company operating out of a winery near Santa Rosa, California. The company specializes in sending California specialties to catalog customers nationwide. Sales are seasonal, with most occurring in November and December—when people select Fresh & Fruity's Famous Fruit Fantasy boxes as Christmas gifts. Although seasonal, the company's sales are fairly predictable, because the bulk of Fresh & Fruity customers are regulars who come back year after year. The company has also managed to smooth out its sales somewhat by offering incentives, such as the Fruit of the Month club, that encourage customers to buy throughout the year.

The nature of the mail-order business is such that most of Fresh & Fruity's sales are on credit; therefore, the company has historically had a high accounts receivable balance relative to sales. It has also historically been short of cash, forcing it to delay payments to suppliers as long as possible (its average time to pay accounts in 2010, was 67 days).

In January 2011, Tom Appleby and Alice Plummer, the president and treasurer of Fresh & Fruity, respectively,

were discussing the cash flow problem over lunch.

"You know, Tom," Alice said as she sliced a piece of avocado, "I was reading the other day about a company called Kringle's Candles & Ornaments, and it occurred to me that we're a lot like them. Most of our assets are current ones like their accounts receivable and inventory; and over half of ours are financed just like theirs, by current liabilities—that is, accounts payable." She paused for a sip of chardonnay, and continued, "They got around their cash flow problems by issuing long-term debt, which took the pressure off their current obligations. I've been looking at that for our company, too; but then I got to thinking, there's another way that's a good deal easier and would produce results just as quickly."

"Oh? What's that?" Tom replied, his interest captured.

"All we have to do," she said, "is to reduce our accounts receivable balance. That will help reduce our accounts payable balance—since, as our customers begin paying us earlier, we can pay our suppliers earlier in turn. If we could get enough customers to pay us right away, we could even pay some of the suppliers in time to take advantage of the 2 percent discount they offer for payments within 10 days." (Fresh & Fruity's suppliers operated on a 2/10, net 60 basis.) "That would increase our net income and free up even more cash to take advantage of even more discounts!" She looked excited at the prospect.

"Sounds great, but how do we get people to pay us earlier?" Tom inquired, doubtfully.

"Easy," Alice continued. "Up to now we've been giving them incentives to pay later. Remember our 'Buy Now, No Payments for Two Months' program? Well, a lot of our customers use it, and it's caused our accounts receivable balance to run way up. So what we have to do now is give them incentives to pay earlier. What I propose is to cancel the buy now/pay later plan and offer a 10 percent discount to everyone who pays with their order, instead."

"But won't that cause our revenues to drop?" Tom asked, again still doubtful.

"Yes, but the drop will be offset by even more new customers who will come in to take advantage of the discount. I figure the net effect on sales will be just about zero, but our accounts receivable balance could be cut in half! Now here's a kicker that I just thought of: After we've reduced our accounts receivable balance as far as practical, I'd like to look into the possibility of reducing our accounts payable still further by replacing them with a bank loan. The effective rate of interest that we pay by not taking our suppliers' discounts is, after all, pretty high. So what I'd like to do is take out a loan once a year of a sufficient size that would enable us to take all the discounts our suppliers offer. The interest that we'll pay on the loan is bound to be less than what we pay in discounts lost—so we'll see another gain in earnings on our income statement. In fact, these two initiatives together might have a really significant impact!"

"You've convinced me," Tom said, "Let's go back to the office and run some figures to see what happens!"

Financial statements for Fresh & Fruity Foods, Inc., are presented in Figure 1 (income statement) and Figure 2 (balance sheet).

Required

1. Using the data in Figures 1 and 2, compute the company's average collection period (ACP) in days. Use a 360-day year when calculating sales per day.

2. Compute the cost, as a percent, that the company is paying for not taking the supplier's discounts. (The supplier's terms are 2/10, net 60; but note from the bottom of Figure 2 that Fresh & Fruity has been taking 67 days to pay its suppliers, making that the effective final due date for accounts payable.)

3. Assume that Alice Plummer's first initiative to offer a 10 percent discount was implemented, and the company's average collection period dropped to 32 days. If *net* sales per day remained the same, as Alice expects, what would be the new accounts receivable balance? How much cash was freed up by the reduction in accounts receivable? What is the new accounts payable balance if the money is used to pay off suppliers?

Figure 1
Current Situation

FRESH & FRUITY FOODS, INC

Income Statement, 2010

Revenue from sales		
Gross sales (credit)		$1,179,000
Cost of goods sold:		
Beginning inventory	$ 141,000	
Purchases $969,000		
Less: Cash discounts....... 0		
Net purchases...	969,000	
Goods available for sale....................................	1,110,000	
Less: Ending inventory	79,557	
Cost of goods sold		1,030,443
Gross profit...		148,557
Selling and administrative expenses		73,000
Earnings before interest and tax...		75,557
Interest expense		0
Earnings before tax		75,557
Income taxes @ 33%..		24,934
Net income...		$ 50,623

Figure 2
Current Situation

FRESH & FRUITY FOODS, INC

Balance Sheet

As of December 31, 2010

Assets:		
Cash	$ 3,560	
Accounts receivable..................................	209,686	
Inventory..	79,557	
Total current assets		$292,803
Property, plant and equipment, net		11,430
Total assets		$304,233
Liabilities and equity:		
Accounts payable......................................	$180,633	
Notes payable (bank loans).......................	0	
Total current liabilities...........................		$180,633
Long-term debt		0
Total liabilities......................................		180,633
Common stock..	13,600	
Additional paid-in capital	83,000	
Retained earnings.....................................	27,000	
Total equity..		123,600
Total liabilities and equity		$304,233
Selected ratios		
Profit Margin	4.29%	
Return on equity	40.96%	
Inventory turnover	14.82	
Receivables turnover	5.62	
Average payment period............................	67	

Required

4. Alice's second initiative calls for Fresh & Fruity to obtain a bank loan of a sufficient size to enable the company to take all suppliers' discounts. What is the minimum size of this loan? (*Hint:* To take all suppliers' discounts, the average payment period must be 10 days, and net purchases will be purchases – (Purchases from Figure 1 x .02). Assume that all this happens, and solve the following formula for the new accounts payable balance, using:

   Accounts payable = Average payment period x Purchase per day*
   *Based on net purchases/360.

   Now compare the accounts payable you just solved with the new accounts payable balance you found in question 3. The difference is the size of the loan that is required.

5. Assume that Fresh &Fruity does obtain an 8 percent loan for one year in the amount you solved in question 5, and it reduces its accounts payable balance accordingly. Now the company is taking 2 percent discounts on all purchases and paying 8 percent a year on the loan balance. What is the net gain from taking the discounts and paying the interest on a before-tax basis? On an aftertax basis?

Optional

6. Suppose the 8 percent loan that Fresh & Fruity obtained was a discount loan, and the bank further required a 20 percent compensating balance of the full loan amount. What is the effective rate of interest to Fresh & Fruity? How does this compare to your answer in question 2 for the cost of not taking a cash discount?

Pierce Control Systems

In 2006, Sam Fenton was extremely pleased to pick up *The Wall Street Journal* and see that the prime rate had fallen to 6 percent. As vice president of finance for Pierce Control Systems, he know he would have to refinance some major long-term debt coming due and he wanted to consider all the possible options.

Pierce Control Systems is a manufacturer of material handling, accessory, and control equipment for the printing industry. Pierce's products are designed to improve the productivity and cost-efficiency of printing presses. Products include automatic cleaning systems, fountain solution and ink control systems, press and web control systems, and web and material handling systems. The business started in 1995 and over the past decade has grown to a sales volume of $40 million.

Sam Fenton had joined the company in 1998. His background included a bachelor's degree in finance and accounting from the University of Memphis, two years with Ernst & Young as an auditor, and a three-year stint with First Wachovia Bank Corporation as a loan officer. After eight years with Pierce Control System, he was promoted to vice president of finance in 2006. At age 36, he was quite proud of his new title and $120,000 salary.

The Financing Decision

With $10 million in debt coming due, Sam Fenton was considering two options. One was to reborrow the money on a five-year basis with Prudential Insurance Company, a major lender to emerging firms. The loan would carry a flat 8 percent rate over the next five years. The principal would be due at the end of the life of the loan.

Sam considered the first option described above as relatively long term in nature. It would ensure that the firm would have adequate financing through 2011. A second option would be to borrow the money from a bank on a short-term basis. Although banks normally lend funds for 90 to 180 day periods, he intended to ask for a one-year loan. He then would renew the loan each year over the five-year period. The loan officer at Bank of America had told Sam that the bank always floats the interest rate on its loans with the prime interest rate. Right now, the prime interest rate was 6 percent or a full 2 percent less than the rate Sam would have to pay on the longer-term insurance company loan.

Furthermore, if Sam maintained compensating balances on 10 percent of the loan outstanding, the interest rate charge would be reduced to ½ percent below prime, or to 5 ½ percent. Clearly, there appeared to be a financial advantage to borrowing the money short term, but Sam also remembered that the prime interest rate could be quite volatile and had reached 20 percent back in 1981. He would look pretty foolish to his boss, William Pierce III, if he were being forced to pay that kind of interest at some point in the future.

Sam Fenton was also concerned about the danger of a future credit crunch in the economy, as was witnessed in 1990 and 1991. At times banks become very hesitant to make loans because of an overabundance of bad loans already on their books and fears of federal regulators criticizing them. This is particularly true when the economy is in a recession and bank loan officers are fearful about future business conditions.

Required

1. Based on the 10 percent compensating balance requirement, how much would Pierce Control Systems have to borrow to acquire $10 million in needed funds?

2. Would the cost of the bank loan with the 10 percent compensating balance requirement and a 5 ½ percent rate applied to the total loan outstanding be more or less than the 6 percent prime rate loan on $10 million? Work this in terms of total dollar interest payments and compare the two answers.

3. What if 4 percent interest could be earned on all funds kept in excess of the $10 million under the compensating balance loan arrangement? What would be the net dollar interest cost of the compensating balance loan arrangement? How does this compare to the 6 percent prime interest rate loan total dollar cost?

4. Based on the difference between the 6 percent prime (short-term) interest rate charged by the bank and the 8 percent longer-term interest rate charged by the insurance company, what does this tell you about the likely current shape of the term structure of interest rates? Based on the expectations hypothesis, what might you infer is the next most likely move in interest rates?

Required

5. Assume the following projected interest rates for the prime rate over the next five years; what would be the total interest cost on the $10 million loan over that period? (Disregard the compensating balance alternative for purposes of this question.) How does this compare to the total dollar cost of the five-year, 8 percent insurance company loan?

	Projected Prime
Year	*Interest Rate*
2007	6%
2008	8%
2009	9%
2010	9%
2011	4%

6. As a second scenario, assume the prime rate would move more dramatically, as shown below:

	Projected Prime
Year	*Interest Rate*
2007	6%
2008	10%
2009	15%
2010	13%
2011	13%

What would be the total dollar cost under the five-year bank loan? How does this compare to the total dollar cost of the five-year insurance company loan?

7. With a probability of 70 percent of the interest rate scenario in question 5 and a 30 percent probability of the interest rate scenario in question 6, what is the expected value of the dollar interest costs of short-term borrowing? Is this higher or lower than the total dollar interest cost of the five-year insurance company loan?

8. At what relative probability between the two scenarios would the firm be indifferent between short-term and long-term borrowing?

9. Briefly explain how hedging can help the firm reduce the risk associated with the short-term borrowing arrangement.

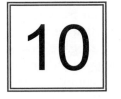

Allison Boone, M.D.

Allison Boone had been practicing medicine for seven years. Her specialty was neurology. She had received her bachelor's degree in chemistry from Kent State University and her M.D. from Washington University in St. Louis. She did her residency at Columbia Presbyterian Hospital in New York. Allison practiced neurology in a clinic with three other doctors in Hurst, Texas.

Her husband, Samuel L. Boone, held an administrative position for Harris Methodist HMO in Arlington, Texas. Allison and Samuel had been married for five years and were parents of young twin sons, Todd and Trey. They lived in Arlington in a beautiful four-room house overlooking Lake Arlington.

Allison normally left for work at 7:30 a.m. and closed her office at 5:30 p.m. to return home. On Tuesday, July 6th, 2006 at 5:15 p.m., she received an emergency call from Arlington General Hospital and immediately went to the hospital to help a patient who had suffered serious brain damage. By the time she had administered aid and helped prepare the patient for surgery it was 11:00 p.m.

On her way home as she passed the Ballpark in Arlington (home of the Texas Rangers baseball team), she was confronted head on by a drunken driver going over 80 miles an hour. A crash was inevitable and Allison and the other driver were killed instantly. The drunken driver was making a late delivery for Wayland Frozen Foods, Inc.

Legal Considerations

The families of both drivers were devastated by the news of the accident. After the funeral and explaining the situation to the children, Samuel Boone knew he must seek legal redress for his family's enormous loss. Following interviews with a number of lawyers, he decided to hire Sloan Whitaker.

Sloan was with a Dallas law firm (Hanson, Sloan, and Thomason) that specialized in plaintiff's lawsuits. He had been in practice for over 20 years since graduating from Southern Methodist University (SMU) law school in 1986.

When Sloan began his investigation on behalf of Samuel Boone and his family, he was surprised to find out the driver of the delivery vehicle had a prior record of alcohol abuse and that Wayland Frozen Foods, Inc. had knowledge of the problem when they hired him. It appears the driver was a relative of the owner and at the time of employment he revealed what he termed "a past alcoholic problem that was now under control". In any event, he was acting as an employee for Wayland Frozen Foods in using their truck to make a business related delivery at the time of the accident. The fact that he was speeding and intoxicated at the time of the impact only increased the legal exposure for Wayland Frozen Foods.

After much negotiating with the law firm that represented Wayland Frozen Foods (and its insurance company), Sloan Whitaker received three proposals for an out-of-court settlement to be paid to Allison Boone's family. The intent of the proposals was to replace the future earning's power of Allison Boone, less any of the earnings she would have personally needed for her normal living requirements. Also, the value that she provided for her family as a wife and mother, quite aside from her earning power, had to be considered. Finally, there was the issue of punitive damages that Wayland Frozen Foods was exposed to as a result of letting an unqualified driver operate its truck. If the case went to court, there was no telling how much a jury might assign to this last factor.

The three proposals are listed below. An actuarial table indicated that Allison, age 37 at the time of the accident, had an anticipated life expectancy of 40 more years.

Proposal 1   Pay the family of Allison Boone $300,000 a year for the next 20 years, and $500,000 a year for the remaining 20 years.

Proposal 2   Pay the family a lump sum payment of $5 million today.

Proposal 3   Pay the family of Allison Boone a relatively small amount of $50,000 a year for the next 40 years, but also guarantee them a final payment of $75 million at the end of 40 years.

In order to analyze the present value of these three proposals, attorney Sloan Whitaker called on a financial expert to do the analysis. You will aid in the process.

Required

1. Assume a discount rate of 6 percent is used, which of the three projects has the highest present value?

   In analyzing the first proposal, take the present value of the 20 year $300,000 annuity. Then take the present value of the deferred annuity of $500,000 that will run from the 21st through the 40th year. The answer you get for the second annuity will represent the value at the beginning of the 21st year (the same as the end of the 20th year). You will need to discount this lump sum value back for 20 years as a single amount to get its present value. You then add together the present value of the first and second annuity.

   The second and third proposals are straight forward and require no further explanation.

2. Now assume that a discount rate of 11 percent is used instead of 6 percent. Which of the three alternatives provides the highest present value?

3. Explain why the change in outcome takes place between question 1 and question 2.

4. If Sloan Whitaker thinks additional punitive damages are likely to be $4 million in a jury trial, should he be more likely to settle out-of-court or go before the jury?

Billy Wilson, All American

In his senior year at a major midwestern university, Billy Wilson had been the third runnerup for the fabled Heismann Trophy. The trophy goes to the outstanding football player in America and is presented annually by the New York Athletic Club. During the past football season, Wilson had run for over 1,500 yards and scored 18 touchdowns. He had also caught 41 passes coming out of the backfield. His time in running the 40-yard dash, which professional scouts consider to be extremely important, was 4.38 seconds. He was voted first team All American by the Associated Press and was a second team All American in the Coaches Poll selections.

On Monday morning, his agent, Joel Weinberg, called to say that he was looking at three different proposals that a major West Coast professional football team had made for Billy Wilson's services. The team had drafted him in the first round of the National Football League draft as the sixth player selected out of the thousands of college football players that were eligible for that year. The Edmonton, Alberta, team of the Canadian Football League was also interested in Wilson's services. The Canadian team had called his agent over the weekend to put its offer on the table. While the NFL (National Football League) team that had drafted Billy Wilson in the first round had exclusive rights over all other U.S. teams to signing Billy Wilson during the current year, the Canadian team was not bound by such an arrangement and could make any offer it wished and hope the outcome would be positive.

Actual Proposals

The West Coast NFL team offered the following three proposals. The team's general manager, who was in charge of contract negotiations, said his team would stand behind any of the three offers and it was up to Billy Wilson and his agent to choose which they preferred.

Contract offer 1:

- $900,000 immediate signing bonus.
- $850,000 at the end of each year for the next five years.

Contract offer 2:

- $200,000 immediate signing bonus.
- $100,000 at the end of each year for the next four years.
- $150,000 a year at the end of years 5 through 10.
- $1,000,000 a year at the end of years 11 through year 40.

Contract offer 3:

- $1,000,000 immediate signing bonus.
- $500,000 at the end of year 1.
- $1,000,000 at the end of year 2.
- $1,500,000 at the end of year 3.
- $2,500,000 at the end of year 4.

As part of the third offer, he was also promised a $200,000 bonus for any year in which he was selected to play in the Pro Bowl All Star game. His agent figured there was a 25 percent probability of that occurring in each of the next four years.

The Edmonton, Alberta, team of the Canadian Football League offered the following:

- $1,100,000 signing bonus.
- $2,000,000 at the end of each year for the next three years.

The Canadian contract was not guaranteed. This means that Billy was assured of his signing bonus, but if he did not make the team in any of the three years, he would not receive his salary. His agent figured there was an 80 percent probability that his contract would be picked up (paid) in each of the next three years. (The U.S. team's contract proposals were all guaranteed.)

Wilson's Reaction

Billy Wilson was a sociology major in college and although he was red-shirted (laid out) for one year, he would still receive his degree at the May graduation ceremonies. He was proud of the 2.75 average (out of 4.0 points) he had compiled because of the rigors of college football. He knew that only about 40 percent of athletes on scholarship ever got their degree. At some schools the average was as low as 10 percent, while Notre Dame boasted about a graduation rate approaching 100 percent.

As a nonbusiness major, Billy was confused about the process for determining the actual numerical value of the offerings. For example, the second contract offer from the U.S. team had a total dollar value of over $31 million. He was astounded by such a figure. He knew that players selected as the *very first player* in the draft in prior years had not received such a high sum. They had been the first players selected in the draft in their respective years, and he was only the sixth player chosen in the current year.

His agent, Joel Weinberg, began to explain to Billy the importance of the time value of money. He said inflows in the future were not worth nearly as much as current inflows and that, therefore, they should be discounted back to the present at a 10 percent interest rate. While Billy did not fully understand how the calculations were done, he knew he could rely on his agent to do the proper analysis.

Required

1. Calculate the present value of the three contract proposals offered by the U.S. team. Factor in any probability considerations where appropriate.
2. Calculate the present value of the contract offered by the Canadian team. Factor in any probability considerations where appropriate.
3. Which of the four contracts offers has the highest present value? What is the amount?
4. If the discount rate used were 7 percent instead of 10 percent, how might that change your answer. You do not need to do new calculations, merely indicate what the likely impact would be.
5. Returning to your answer for question 3, assume Billy Wilson's agent will receive 10 percent of the present value of the contract as his fee. Also, the remaining 90 percent will be taxed at 33 percent. What is the aftertax value of the present value of the proceeds that Billy will receive?
6. If Billy and his agent think tax rates are likely to be higher in the future, how might that influence the decision?
7. Using the answer from question 3, how large an annuity could Billy Wilson pay himself for the next 40 years at 10 percent interest?
8. What other factors should Billy Wilson consider?

CASE

Gilbert Enterprises

Tom Gilbert, founder and chairman of the board of Gilbert Enterprises, could not believe his eyes as he read the quote about his firm in *The Wall Street Journal*. The stock had closed at 35 1/4, down 3 3/4 points for the week. He called his Vice President of Finance, Jane Arnold, and they agreed to meet on Saturday morning at 9:00 a.m. for breakfast.

When Jane arrived, they reviewed the stock's performance for the last few months. Although the stock opened the year (2006) at 28 ½ per share, it had reached a high of 50 in March, but had steadily slid in value to its current level of 35 1/4 in mid-May. Tom and Jane both thought the stock was undervalued in the marketplace and were seriously considering an announcement that the firm was going to repurchase up to one million of its own shares in the open market beginning on June 1st of 2006. They thought that would send a message to investors that the market had placed the stock at an unrealistically low level.

Before taking any action, they decided to consult with their investment banking representative, Albert Roth, senior vice president at the investment banking firm of Baker, Green and Roth. Roth had aided the firm in initially selling its stock to the public (going public) five years ago and was quite familiar with its operations. Although he was surprised to receive their call during an early Saturday morning round of golf at the country club, he promised to get back with them in the next few days with his recommendations on a stock repurchase.

The Firm's Business

Gilbert Enterprises was the third largest firm in the auto parts replacement industry, specializing in brake parts, power transmissions, batteries, cables and other products related to used automobiles. Although most auto industry advertising relates to flashy new cars, Albert Roth knew that the auto parts replacement industry was becoming increasingly important.

His research indicated that the average age of an automobile life had reached eight years in 2006, up from a mere 6.8 years in the mid-1980's. Why? New vehicle price increases had far surpassed the rise in consumer income. People are now forced to keep their old cars longer whether they want to or not. Furthermore, 1990 (and other legislation) has mandated more emission inspections and maintenance programs. Consumers are now being forced to spend more money to update older automobiles to meet these standards.

Valuation

Gilbert Enterprises had the most advanced just-in-time (JIT) inventory management system in the industry. For that reason, Albert Roth believed the firm would enjoy supernormal growth beyond industry standards for the next three years. His best estimate was that a 15 percent growth rate during that time period was entirely reasonable. After that time span, a more normal growth rate of 6 percent was expected. Because of the supernormal growth potential, he decided to consult Appendix 10C of the Block and Hirt textbook to compute the value. Current dividends (D_0) were 1.20 per share and he decided to use a discount or required rate of return (K_e) of 10 percent.

He discussed this approach with his partners and while they generally agreed, they suggested that he also consider a more traditional approach of comparing the firm's price-earnings ratio to other firms in the industry. Price-earnings data along with other information are shown in Figure 1 for Gilbert Enterprises and three other firms in the industry.

Figure 1

Comparative Data for Auto Parts Replacement Firms

	Gilbert Enterprises	Reliance Parts	Standard Auto	Allied Motors
Annual Growth in EPS (last 5 years)	12%	8%	7%	9%
Return on Stockholders' Equity	18.0%	25.3%	14.0%	15.3%
Return on Total Assets	12.1%	8.1%	10.5%	9.8%
Debt to Total Assets	33%	68%	25%	36%
Market Value	$35.25	$70.50	$24.25	$46.75
Book Value	$16.40	$50.25	$19.50	$50.75
Replacement Value	$43.50	$68.75	$26.00	$37.50
Dividend Yield	3.40%	2.18%	5.26%	3.12%
P/E ratio	16.8	24.1	14.2	18.1

Required

1. Using the approach for the valuation of a supernormal growth firm as shown in Appendix 10C of the textbook, compute the value of Gilbert Enterprises' stock. Round all values in the computation to two places to the right of the decimal point. Does the firm appear to be under or overvalued?

2. Examine the data in Figure 1 and indicate whether the firm's P/E ratio appears to be appropriate in light of other firms in the industry.

3. Based on the answers to questions 1 and 2, what recommendation would you suggest that Albert Roth make?

CASE

Baines Investments, Inc.

Baines Investments, Inc. is a private equity investment company located in Dallas, Texas. The firm specializes in investing in privately owned firms that it feels it can sell in the future at a higher price or eventually take public. In most cases, the firm engages in leveraged buyouts, in which it borrows money to buy a publicly traded company with the intention of taking it private. After restructuring the firm by selling off unnecessary assets and tightening budgets to increase profitability, Baines Investments and other participating investing firms eventually hope to take the company back to the public market at a much higher price than they paid to take it private.

An Upcoming Deal

Joel Horlen recently received his MBA from Baylor University and was hired by Baines Investment, Inc. In his first six months on the job, he assisted other analysts in evaluating companies, but now he had an assignment of his own.

The company he was to assess is United Defense Systems (UDS). The firm manufactures warships and cargo ships for the U.S. government. It also produces automatic flight control radar systems and intercept missiles. It is privately traded.

Joel's firm normally took the present value of future dividends, earnings, or cash flow to determine value. In Joel's first analysis he decided to take the present value of future dividends. Because dividends appeared to be growing at a constant rate for the foreseeable future, he decided to use the constant growth rate dividend valuation model in which the price (P_0) or value was equal to

$$P_0 = \frac{D_1}{K_e - g}$$

A careful analysis of company data indicated that D_1, or the next period's dividend would be $1.80. The growth rate g appeared to be 5.5 percent. K_e was supposed to represent the cost of common equity and was normally given to him in his classroom exercises while working on his MBA. However, his employer, Baines Investment, Inc., insisted that he use the capital asset pricing model to compute the cost (or required return) on common equity.

The term K_e in the formula above represents the cost of common equity, but can easily be replaced by K_j, the required return on common equity under the capital asset pricing model. Once K_j is computed it is merely substituted for K_e in the prior formula.

Now the formula for K_j.

$$K_j \text{ is equal to } R_f + \beta(K_m - R_f)$$

where:

K_j	=	Required return on common stock
R_f	=	Risk-free rate – use 6%
K_m	=	Market rate of return – use 11%
β	=	Beta. The volatility of a stock's return relative to the market's return.
		To be determined.

A stock with a beta of one would be as volatile as the market. A stock with a beta of 1.20 would be 20 percent more volatile than the market, and a stock with a beta of .80 would be 20 percent less volatile than the market and so on. The beta was normally computed over a five-year period for a publicly traded company.

Because the company (UDS) that Joel Horlen was evaluating was private and had no public stock price, Joel decided to use an alternative method to compute beta. He would take the average beta of five publicly traded companies in the same industry as UDS (Aerospace/defense). The betas for the five companies are as follows:

Company	Beta
Armour Holdings	1.40
BE Aerospace	1.65
General Dynamics	.85
Lockheed Martin	.80
Northrop Gruman	.80

Required

1. Compute the average beta for the five firms in the aerospace/defense industry.

2. Now, compute the required rate of return (K_j) using the capital asset pricing model. R_f is equal to 6 percent and K_m is equal to 11 percent.
   Use the formula:
   K_j is equal to $R_f + \beta(K_m - R_f)$.

3. Next, compute the stock price (P_0) using the formula:
   $$P_0 = \frac{D_1}{K_j - g}$$
   Note K_j (the required return on common stock) is being substituted for K_e (the cost of common equity). They both represent the same thing, the return that stockholders demand.

4. Using your answer from question 3 and assuming earnings per share are $2.40, what is the P/E ratio?

5. Because the firm is privately held and thus there is no public market for its securities, there will be a liquidity discount of 20 percent from the stock price computed in question 3. What will the adjusted stock price be? What will the adjusted P/E be?

6. Assume that Joel Horlen discovers that UDS is about to win a major new defense department contract on combat radar systems and the Company's value will increase by 40 percent. Ignoring the liquidity discount for this calculation, what will the new stock price and P/E ratio be?

7. Discuss the impact of the company deciding to go public sometime in the future on the liquidity discount.

14

Atlantic Airlines

Atlantic Airlines issued $100 million in bonds in 2008. Because of the firm's low credit rating (B3), the bonds were considered to be junk bonds. At the time of issue, the 20 year bonds were paying a yield of 12 percent.

Investor Tom Phillips thought the yield on the bonds was particularly attractive and called his broker, Roger Brown, to ask for more information on the debt issue. Tom currently held Treasury bonds paying four percent interest and corporate bonds yielding six percent. He wondered why the debt issue of Atlantic Airlines was paying twice that of his other corporate bonds and eight percent more than Treasury securities.

His broker, Roger Brown had been a financial consultant with Merrill Lynch for 10 years and was frequently asked such questions about yield. He explained to Tom that the bonds were not considered investment grade because of the industry they were in. Bonds of airlines are considered to be inherently risky because of exposure to volatile energy prices and the high debt level that many airlines carry. He further explained that they frequently were labeled "junk bonds" because their rating did not fall into the four highest categories of ratings by the bond rating agencies of Moody's and Standard and Poor's.

Questions from Tom Phillips

This explanation did not deter Tom from showing continued interest. In fact, he could hardly wait to get his hands on the 12 percent yielding securities. But first, he asked Roger, "What is the true risk and is it worth taking?"

Roger explained there was a higher risk of default on junk bonds. It sometimes ran as high as 2-3 percent during severe economic downturns (compared to .5 percent for more conventional issues). Roger also indicated that although the yield at the time of issue appeared high, it could go considerably higher should conditions worsen in the airline industry. This would take place if the price of oil moved sharply upward or people began flying less due to a downturn in the economy. Roger explained that if the yield (required return) on bonds of this nature went up, the price of the bonds would go down and could potentially wipe out the high interest payment advantage.

Required

1. If the yield in the market for bonds of this nature were to go up to 15 percent due to poor economic conditions, what would the new price of the bonds be? They have an initial par value of $1,000. Assume two years have passed and there are 18 years remaining on the life of the bonds. Use annual analysis.

2. Compare the decline in value to the eight percent initial interest advantage over Treasury bonds (12 percent versus four percent) for this two year holding period. Base your analysis on a $1,000 bond. Disregarding tax considerations, would Tom come out ahead or behind in buying the high yield bonds?

3. Recompute the price of the bonds if interest rates went up by only one percent to 13 percent with 18 years remaining. Does the 8 percent interest rate advantage over the two year holding period cover the loss in value?

4. Now assume that economic conditions improve and the yield on similar securities goes down by 2 or 3 percent over the two years. How does Tom come out? Merely discuss the answer. No calculation is necessary.

5. If Tom holds the bonds to maturity (and there is no default), does the change in the required yield in the market over the life of the bond have any direct effect on the investment?

Berkshire Instruments

Al Hansen, the newly appointed vice president of finance of Berkshire Instruments, was eager to talk to his investment banker about future financing for the firm. One of Al's first assignments was to determine the firm's cost of capital. In assessing the weights to use in computing the cost of capital, he examined the current balance sheet, presented in Figure 1.

In their discussion, Al and his investment banker determined that the current mix in the capital structure was very close to optimal and that Berkshire Instruments should continue with it in the future. Of some concern was the appropriate cost to assign to each of the elements in the capital structure. Al Hansen requested that his administrative assistant provide data on what the cost to issue debt and preferred stock had been in the past. The information is provided in Figure 2.

When Al got the data, he felt he was making real progress toward determining the cost of capital for the firm. However, his investment banker indicated that he was going about the process in an incorrect manner. The important issue is the current cost of funds, not the historical cost. The banker suggested that a comparable firm in the industry, in terms of size and bond rating (Baa), Rollins Instruments, had issued bonds a year and a half ago for 9.3 percent interest at a $1,000 par value, and the bonds were currently selling for $890. The bonds had 20 years remaining to maturity. The banker also observed that Rollings Instruments had just issued preferred stock at $60 per share, and the preferred stock paid an annual dividend of $4.80.

In terms of cost of common equity, the banker suggested that Al Hansen use the dividend valuation model as a first approach to determining cost of equity. Based on that approach, Al observed that earnings were $3 a share and that 40 percent would be paid out in dividends (D_1). The current stock price was $25. Dividends in the last four years had grown from 82 cents to the current value.

The banker indicated that the underwriting cost (flotation cost) on a preferred stock issue would be $2.60 per share and $2.00 per share on common stock. Al Hansen further observed that his firm was in a 35 percent marginal tax bracket.

With all this information in hand, Al Hansen sat down to determine his firm's cost of capital. He was a little confused about computing the firm's cost of common equity. He knew there were two different formulas: one: one for the cost of retained earnings and one for the cost of new common stock. His investment banker suggested that he follow the normally accepted approach used in determining the marginal cost of capital. First, determine the cost of capital for as large a capital structure as current retained earnings will support; then, determine the cost of capital based on exclusively using new common stock.

Figure 1

BERKSHIRE INSTRUMENTS
Statement of Financial Position
December 31, 2010

Assets

Current assets:

Cash		$ 400,000
Marketable securities		200,000
Accounts receivable	$ 2,600,000	
Less: Allowance for bad debts	300,000	2,300,000
Inventory		5,500,000
Total current assets		$ 8,400,000

Fixed Assets:

Plant and equipment, original cost	30,700,000	
Less: Accumulated depreciation	13,200,000	
Net plant and equipment		17,500,000
Total assets		$25,900,000

Liabilities and Stockholders' Equity

Current liabilities:

Accounts payable	$ 6,200,000
Accrued expenses	1,700,000
Total current liabilities	7,900,000

Long-term financing:

Bonds payable	$ 6,120,000
Preferred stock	1,080,000
Common stock }Common equity	6,300,000
Retained earnings	4,500,000
Total common equity	10,800,000
Total long-term financing	18,000,000
Total liabilities and stockholders' equity	$25,900,000

Figure 2
Cost of prior issues of debt and preferred stock

Security	Year of Issue	Amount	Coupon Rate
Bond	1998	$1,120,000	6.1%
Bond	2002	3,000,000	13.8
Bond	2008	2,000,000	8.3
Preferred stock.............................	2003	600,000	12.0
Preferred stock.............................	2006	480,000	7.9

Required

1. Determine the weighted average cost of capital based on using retained earnings in the capital structure. The percentage composition in the capital structure for bonds, preferred stock, and common equity should be based on the current capital structure of long-term financing as shown in Figure 1 (it adds up to $18 million). Common equity will represent 60 percent of financing throughout this case. Use Rollins instruments data to calculate the cost of preferred stock and debt.

2. Recompute the weighted average cost of capital based on using new common stock in the capital structure. The weights remain the same, only common equity is now supplied by new common stock, rather than by retained earnings. After how much new financing will this increase in the cost of capital take place? Determine this by dividing retained earnings by the percent of common equity in the capital structure.

3. Assume the investment banker also wishes to use the capital asset pricing model, as shown in Formula 11.5 in the text, to compute the cost (required return) on common stock. Assume $R_f = 6$ percent, ß is 1.25, and K_m is 13 percent. What is the value of K_j? How does this compare to the value of K_e computed in question 1?

Galaxy Systems, Inc.

As the three division managers of Galaxy systems, Inc. entered the central headquarters meeting room each felt under pressure. They were there to meet with Marlene Davidson, the senior vice president of finance.

Marlene, a CPA who had spent seven years with Ernst and Young before being recruited by Galaxy Systems, was a strong believer in implementing the latest techniques in corporate financial management.

She maintained that there should not be one figure for cost of capital that was uniformly applied throughout the corporation. Although the current figure of 12 percent was well documented, she intended to propose that different types of investments utilize different discount rates. Her first inclination was to suggest that the nature of the project be the controlling factor in determining the discount rate. The riskier the project the higher the discount rate required. For example, repair to old machinery might carry a discount rate of six percent; a new product, 12 percent; and investments in foreign markets, 20 percent. This was a well accepted method that she had used a number of times while on consulting assignments at Ernst and Young.

When she discussed this approach with Joe Halstead, the CEO of Galaxy Systems, he said the risk-adjusted discount rate made a lot of sense to him. He went on to say that management as well as stockholders tend to be risk averse and, therefore, higher risk projects should meet tougher return standards.

However, in the case of Galaxy Systems, Mr. Halstead suggested they consider a slightly different approach. He maintained that his company was made up of three distinctly different businesses and that each business should have its own imputed rate to be used as its discount rate.

The three divisions were a) the airline parts manufacturing division; b) the auto airbags production division, and c) the aerospace division. The latter division built modern missile and control systems and jet fighter planes under contract with the defense department of the U.S. government.

Mr. Halstead maintained that each division had a risk dimension that was uniquely its own. He asked Marlene Davidson about a strategy to measure risk exposure for each division. She suggested that there were two major approaches to do this.

A. Find comparable public companies in each industry the division was in and look up their betas.[*] The higher the average beta for a given industry, the more risk the comparable companies in that industry had. Divisions that were in industries with high average betas would have higher required rates of return.

B. A second approach would not rely on betas for comparable companies to the division, but rather would utilize internal data for that division. The more volatile the *division's* annual earnings relative to the *company's* annual earnings, the riskier the division and the higher the required rate of return.

The Meeting

CEO Joe Halstead liked these ideas and suggested that Marlene Davidson present them to the division managers. After the usual social patter following their arrival at central headquarters, Marlene laid her ideas on the table. At first, the division managers seemed somewhat shocked at her proposals. Marlene had not realized the extent that "empire building" had developed over the years. The three division managers clearly were apprehensive about what discount rate (sometimes referred to as a hurdle rate) would be assigned to their divisions.

The head of the airline parts manufacturing division argued against the use of the betas of publicly traded companies to determine risk. He said there were very few companies that were exclusively engaged in the manufacturing of airline parts. Most of his competitors were subsidiaries of other large companies such as McDonnell Douglas or Ratheon, which were involved in numerous activities. He argued that using the betas of such multi-industry firms and applying them to his division to determine risk would be unfair.

The head of the auto airbags production division had another concern. His three plants were all located in California and the state had tough environmental laws. About one out of every five investments in his division were mandatory under California law.

Finally, the head of the aerospace division said that risk should not be the key variable for determining the divisional discount rates. He suggested that the key consideration in determining the discount rate should be the perceived importance of the division to the corporation. He said "Galaxy Systems was founded as an aerospace company and our future should be tied to our heritage." Approximately 40 percent of Galaxy Systems revenues and earnings were currently tied to the aerospace division, while the other two divisions split the remainder of sales and income almost evenly.

---

[*]As described in Chapter 11, the beta measures the historical volatility of an individual stock's return to the stock market in general. The typical stock has a beta of one. That is, it is as volatile as the market. Stocks that move more rapidly than the market might have a beta of 1.3 (30% more volatile than the market). Other less volatile stocks might have a beta of only .7.

The Initial Decision

After receiving the input from her boss and the three division heads, Marlene Davidson decided to go with the following system. The weighted average cost of capital of 12 percent for the entire corporation would be the starting point for the corporation.

The airline parts manufacturing division would continue to use 12 percent as its discount rate.

Because firms comparable to the auto airbags production division had an average beta* of .8 and the division itself had less variable earnings from year to year than the corporation, it would be assigned a discount rate of 10 percent.

The head of the aerospace division was displeased to be assigned a discount rate of 15 percent. Marlene Davidson justified the high hurdle rate on the basis of an average beta of 1.35 in the aerospace industry and the highly risky business of dealing with the government. Contracts were often cut back when a new administration came into power.

Application of Divisional Hurdle Rates

The application of the new system got its first test when the auto airbags production division and the aerospace division simultaneously submitted four proposals.

Proposal A

The auto airbags production division submitted a proposal for a new airbag model that would cost $2,355,600 to develop. The anticipated revenue stream for the next 10 years was $400,000 per year.

Proposal B

The aerospace division proposed the development of new radar surveillance equipment. The anticipated cost was $2,441,700. The anticipated revenue stream for this project was $450,000 per year for the next 10 years.

Proposal C

Proposal C was a second proposal from the auto airbags division. It called for special equipment to be used in the disposal of environmentally harmful waste material created in the manufacturing process. The equipment cost $145,680 and was expected to provide cost savings of $15,000 per year for 15 years.

Proposal D

Proposal D was a second proposal from the aerospace division. It called for the development of a new form of a microelectric control system that could be used for fighter jets that were still in the design stage at another aerospace company. If the other aerospace company was successful in the development of the fighter jets, they would be sold to underdeveloped countries in various sectors of the world. The cost to produce the microelectric control system was $1,262,100 and the best guess estimate was that the investment would return $300,000 a year for the next eight years.

Required

1. Compute the internal rate of return and the net present value for each of these four proposals.
2. Based strictly on the calculations, which proposals should be accepted or rejected. Use the appropriate divisional discount rate. The net present value provides the answer directly while the internal rate of return must be compared to the discount rate (which is the same as the required rate of return).
3. What subjective elements might override or influence any of the answers provided to Question 2.
4. Assume the head of the aerospace division asked for a second review on the new radar surveillance equipment (Proposal B). He maintains that the numbers presented in Proposal B are correct, but he wants you, the analyst, to know that $300,000 has already been spent on the initial research on this project. (It's not included in the $2,441,700). He suggests that this might influence your decision. What should be your response?

17

Aerocomp, Inc.

As she headed toward her boss's office, Emily Hamilton, chief operating officer for the Aerocomp Corporation—a computer services firm that specialized in airborne support—wished she could remember more of her training in financial theory that she had been exposed to in college. Emily had just completed summarizing the financial aspects of four capital investment projects that were open to Aerocomp during the coming year, and she was faced with the task of recommending which should be selected. What concerned her was the knowledge that her boss, Kay Marsh, a "street smart" chief executive, with no background in financial theory, would immediately favor the project that promised the highest gain in reported net income. Emily knew that selecting projects purely on that basis would be incorrect; but she wasn't sure of her ability to convince Kay, who tended to assume financiers thought up fancy methods just to show how smart they were.

As she prepared to enter Kay's office, Emily pulled her summary sheets from her briefcase and quickly reviewed the details of the four projects, all of which she considered to be equally risky.

A. A proposal to add a jet to the company's fleet. The plane was only six years old and was considered a good buy at $300,000. In return, the plane would bring over $600,000 in additional revenue during the next five years with only about $56,000 in operating costs. (See Figure 1 for details.)

B. A proposal to diversify into copy machines. The franchise was to cost $700,000, which would be amortized over a 40-year period. The new business was expected to generate over $1.4 million in sales over the next five years, and over $800,000 in aftertax earnings. (See Figure 2 for details.)

C. A proposal to buy a helicopter. The machine was expensive and, counting additional training and licensing requirements, would cost $40,000 a year to operate. However, the versatility that the helicopter was expected to provide would generate over $1.5 million in additional revenue, and it would give the company access to a wider market as well. (See Figure 3 for details.)

D. A proposal to begin operating a fleet of trucks. Ten could be bought for only $51,000 each, and the additional business would bring in almost $700,000 in new sales in the first two years alone. (See Figure 4 for details).

In her mind, Emily quickly went over the evaluation methods she had used in the past: payback, internal rate of return, and net present value. Emily knew that Kay would add a fourth, size of reported earnings, but she hoped she could talk Kay out of using it this time. Emily herself favored the net present value method, but she had always had a tough time getting Kay to understand it.

One additional constraint that Emily had to deal with was Kay's insistence that no outside financing be used this year. Kay was worried that the company was growing too fast and had piled up

Figure 1   Financial analysis of Project A: Add a twin-jet to the company's fleet

	Initial Expenditures	*Year 1*	*Year 2*	*Year 3*	*Year 4*	*Year 5*
Net cost of new plane	$300,000					
Additional revenue		$43,000	$76,800	$112,300	$225,000	$168,750
Additional operating costs.........		11,250	11,250	11,250	11,250	11,250
Depreciation		45,000	66,000	63,000	63,000	63,000
Net increase in income		(13,250)	(450)	38,050	150,750	94,500
Less: Tax at 33%		0	0	12,557	49,748	31,185
Increase in aftertax income........		($13,250)	($ 450)	$ 25,494	$101,003	$ 63,315
Add back depreciation...............		$45,000	$66,000	$ 63,000	63,000	$ 63,000
Net change in cash flow .... ($300,000)		31,750	65,550	88,494	164,003	126,315

Figure 2   Financial analysis of Project B: Diversify into copy machines

	Initial Expenditures	*Year 1*	*Year 2*	*Year 3*	*Year 4*	*Year 5*
Net cost of new franchise	$700,000					
Additional revenue		$ 87,500	$175,000	$262,500	$393,750	$525,000
Additional operating costs.........		26,250	26,250	26,250	26,250	26,250
Amortization..............................		17,500	17,500	17,500	17,500	17,500
Net increase in income		43,750	131,250	218,750	350,000	481,250
Less: Tax at 33%		14,438	43,313	72,188	115,500	158,813
Increase in aftertax income........		$ 29,313	$ 87,938	$146,563	$234,500	$322,438
Add back depreciation...............		$ 17,500	$ 17,500	$ 17,500	$ 17,500	$ 17,500
Net change in cash flow .... ($700,000)		46,813	105,438	164,063	252,000	339,938

enough debt for the time being. She was also against a stock issue for fear of diluting earnings and her control over the firm. As a result of Kay's prohibition of outside financing, the size of the capital budget this year was limited to $800,000, which meant that only one of the four projects under consideration could be chosen. Emily wasn't too happy about that, either, but she had decided to accept it for now, and concentrate on selecting the best of the four.

As she closed her briefcase and walked toward Kay's door, Emily reminded herself to have patience; Kay might not trust financial analysis, but she would listen to sensible arguments. Emily only hoped her financial analysis sounded sensible!

Figure 3   Financial analysis of Project C: Add a helicopter to the company's fleet

	Initial Expenditures	*Year 1*	*Year 2*	*Year 3*	*Year 4*	*Year 5*
Net cost of helicopter................	$800,000					
Additional revenue		$100,000	$200,000	$300,000	$450,000	$600,000
Additional operating costs		40,000	40,000	40,000	40,000	40,000
Depreciation		120,000	176,000	168,000	168,000	168,000
Net increase in income..............		(60,000)	(16,000)	92,000	242,000	392,000
Less: Tax at 33%		0	0	30,360	79,860	129,360
Increase in aftertax income.......		($ 60,000)	($ 16,000)	$ 61,640	$162,140	$262,640
Add back depreciation		$120,000	$ 176,000	$168,000	$168,000	$168,000
Net change in cash flow............	($800,000)	60,000	160,000	229,640	330,140	430,640

Figure 4   Financial analysis of Project D: Add fleet of trucks

	Initial Expenditures	*Year 1*	*Year 2*	*Year 3*	*Year 4*	*Year 5*
Net cost of new trucks	$510,000					
Additional revenue		$382,500	$325,125	$ 89,250	$ 76,500	$ 51,000
Additional operating costs		19,125	19,125	25,500	31,875	38,250
Depreciation		76,500	112,200	107,100	107,100	107,100
Net increase in income..............		286,875	193,800	(43,350)	(62,475)	(94,350)
Less: Tax at 33%		94,669	63,954	0	0	0
Increase in aftertax income.......		$192,206	$129,846	($ 43,350)	($ 62,475)	($ 94,350)
Add back depreciation		$ 76,500	$112,200	$107,100	107,100	$107,100
Net change in cash flow............	($510,000)	268,706	242,046	63,750	44,625	12,750

Required

1. Refer to Figures 1 through 4. Add up the total increase in aftertax income for each project. Given what you know about Kay Marsh, to which project do you think she will be attracted?

2. Compute the payback period, internal rate of return (IRR), and net present value (NPV) of all four alternatives based on cash flow. Use 10 percent for the cost of capital in your calculations. For the payback method, merely indicate the year in which the cash flow equals or exceeds the initial investment. You do not have to compute midyear points.

3. *a.* According to the payback method, which project should be selected?

    b. What is the chief disadvantage of this method?

    c. Why would anyone want to use this method?

4. *a.* According to the IRR method, which project should be chosen?

    b. What is the major disadvantage of the IRR method that occurs when high IRR projects are selected?

    c. Can you think of another disadvantage of the IRR method?
    (*Hint:* Look over the four alternatives and compare the sizes of the projects. Ask yourself whether you would prefer to make a large percent return on a small amount of money or a small percent gain on a large amount of money.)

    d. If Kay had not put a limit on the size of the capital budget, would the IRR method allow acceptance of all four alternatives? If not, which one(s) would be rejected and why?

5. *a.* According to the NPV method, which project should be chosen? How does this differ from the answer under the IRR?

    b. If Kay had not put a limit on the size of the capital budget, under the NPV method which projects would be accepted? Do the NPV and IRR both reject the same project(s)? Why?

    c. Given all the facts of the case, are you more likely to select Project A or C?

18

Phelps Toy Company

The Phelps Toy Company was considering the advisability of adding a new product to its line. Ike Barnes was in charge of new product development. Since the founding of the company in 1990, he had seen sales grow from $150,000 a year to almost $40 million in 2010. Although the firm had initially started out manufacturing toy trucks, it had diversified into such items as puzzles, stuffed animals, wall posters, miniature trains, and board games. In 2004, it developed the third most popular board game for the year, based on a popular television quiz show, but the show was canceled two years later. Nevertheless, the firm learned its lesson well and continued to produce board games related not only to quiz shows but to situation comedies and even a popular detective series.

However, by January of 2011, the need to generate new products was becoming evident. As can be seen in Figure 1, sales and net income were beginning to level off after the previously cited phenomenal growth. After doing a market analysis of possible products, Mr. Barnes decided that the baseball card market was a good area for potential new sales. Baseball cards were a popular product not only among youngsters but also among adults who were trying to recapture the experience of their youth.

A market survey by Ikes Barnes indicated that the Topps Chewing Gum Company was the largest competitor in the industry. The company actually had a public distribution of its common stock in 2003. Other major sellers in 2011 were Upper Deck, Fleer, Leaf, and Donruss. All produce millions of baseball cards on an annual basis. The cards can be purchased in packs of 15–20 cards for $1.00–$3.00 at drug or convenience stores* or in boxes of 700-800 cards for $20 and up. These larger quantities of cards were usually purchased from sport card specialty stores or at baseball card conventions (over 1,000 such conventions throughout the country took place a year).

In doing his analysis, Mr. Barnes discovered that the appeal of baseball cards was not only in opening a wrapper and finding a favorite player enclosed but also that any baseball cards initially purchased for pennies had gained substantially in value. Once a player achieved star status, his rookie card (first issued) might greatly increase in worth.

*Some packs are more expensive than others due to quality and buyer preference.

Figure 1
Phelps Toy Company

Year	Sales	Net Income
1992	$ 150,000	$ (16,000)
1993	240,000	(5,000)
1994	756,000	72,000
1995	1,340,000	91,000
1996	2,680,000	175,000
1997	3,320,000	198,000
1998	5,580,000	248,000
1999	6,792,000	387,000
2000	5,941,000	291,000
2001	9,237,000	439,000
2002	11,622,000	566,000
2003	12,140,000	621,000
2004	17,165,000	850,000
2005	22,838,000	1,221,000
2006	27,762,000	1,437,000
2007	32,437,000	1,628,000
2008	38,911,000	1,762,000
2009	39,750,000	2,002,000
2010	39,860,000	1,950,000

For example, the 1968 rookie card of Nolan Ryan was selling for $2,000 in early 2010. The 1963 Pete Rose rookie card was valued at $500 and, finally, the first Topps card of Mickey Mantle issued in 1952 at 1 cent carried a trading value of $30,000 five decades later. While the card manufacturer did not directly participate in this price appreciation, the hope for such gains in the future keeps youngsters and adults continually active in buying cards as they come out.

To convince management that the manufacturing and selling of baseball cards was a suitable activity for his firm, Mr. Barnes had to make a thorough capital budgeting analysis for the executive committee of Phelps Toy Company.

The Analysis

In evaluating the market potential, Mr. Barnes determined that there was no way he could firmly predict the market penetration potential for a new set of baseball cards.

The sales for the set, which would be called Baseball Stars, would depend on the quality of the final product as well as the effectiveness of the promotional activities. There is also the danger of a number of errors when a set is initially issued. With approximately 750 cards in the set, there is the possibility of misquoting batting averages, misspelling names, and so on. When Fleer and Donruss introduced their new sets in 1995, they were highly criticized by collectors for the numerous errors. Mr. Barnes hoped to avoid this fate for the Baseball Stars set by making heavy expenditures on quality control. He also intended to hire a number of employees from other card companies so he would have experienced people who could identify potential problems at a very early stage.

Over the years, Phelps Toy Company had developed a manual to evaluate capital budgeting projects. As a first step, Ike Barnes was required to predict anticipated sales over the next six years. While he thought this was too short a time period to evaluate the full potential of the project, he knew he had no choice but to go along with company policy. He decided to project a range for potential sales in 2011 (the first new year of business) and assign probabilities to the outcomes. The information is shown in Figure 2.

Figure 2
Projected first-year sales

Assumption	Sales	Probability
Pessimistic	$1,100,000	0.25
Normal	2,000,000	0.40
Optimistic	3,750,000	0.20
Highly optimistic	4,500,000	0.15
		1.00

It was his intention to determine the expected value for sales for the first year and then project a 20 percent growth rate for the next three years and 10 percent for the final two years. Operating expenses, which were expected to average 70 percent of sales, would then be subtracted to determine earnings before depreciation and taxes. The primary investment to be made was in printing and production equipment, which would fall into the five-year MACRS depreciation category. The equipment, which represents the investment for the project, costs $2.8 million.

Mr. Barnes looked into the capital budgeting manual to determine the appropriate discount rate (as shown in Figure 3). The discount rate for the project is based on the coefficient of variation of the first year's sales. One of the accounting assistants informed him that the standard deviation of first year's sales was $1,226,000. He knew he could easily determine the expected value from the data previously presented (in Figure 2).

Mr. Barnes thought that it was now time to call his assistants together to do the appropriate analysis.

Figure 3
Discount rate determination

Coefficient of Variation	Discount Rate
0–.20	8%
.21–.40	10
.41–.60	14
.61–.80	16
Over .80	20

Required

1. Use the basic data in the case to put together an analysis similar to Table 12.11 in the text. To determine earnings before depreciation and taxes (EBDT), subtract projected operating expenses from projected sales. Use a tax rate of 34 percent.
2. Determine the appropriate discount rate for the firm.
3. Make a decision on whether the project is feasible, based on net present value analysis.
4. What is the drawback to using a six-year time horizon for the project?

CASE

Global Resources

Roger Mills, the Vice President of Finance of Global Resources, was concerned about the fact that Global Resources used one discount rate to evaluate all projects. Currently that rate was 10 percent. He knew certain projects were riskier than others, and he felt they should carry a higher discount rate (hurdle rate) than more conservative projects.

The firm had just hired Jennifer Morrison, an MBA from the Wharton School at the University of Pennsylvania (at a starting salary of 150,000 a year). Roger felt with her education and training, she should be able to provide some meaningful suggestions.

Jennifer said, "There are several ways to account for risk in the capital budgeting process, but the most widely used method by Fortune 500 companies is the risk-adjusted discount rate approach. You set up different risk categories in the corporate capital budgeting manual and specify an appropriate discount rate for each."

One of the case studies she had used at the Wharton school actually specified risk categories as shown in Figure 1. Jennifer also added discount rates based on the risk level that might be appropriate for Global Resources.

Figure 1

Risk-Adjusted Discount Rates for Global Resources

Risk Category	Discount Rate
Low risk (equipment repair)	5%
Low to moderate risk (new equipment)	7%
Moderate risk (expansion of product line)	10%
Moderate to high risk (new product in the domestic market)	13%
Risky (established product in a foreign market)	17%
High risk (new product in a foreign market)	20%

She proposed that Roger compare the current method and the risk-adjusted discount rate approach based on two pending proposals. Project A called for introducing a new high grade fuel in the domestic market and would require a discount rate of 13 percent based on Figure 1. Project B called for the introduction of a well-established automatic wheel adjustor in the Asian markets and would require a discount rate of 17 percent based on Figure 1.

The cash flows from the two projects are shown in Figure 2.

Figure 2

Risk-Adjusted Discount Rates for Global Resources

Investment A		Investment B	
($200,000 investment)		($200,000 investment)	
Year	Inflows	Year	Inflows
1	$40,000	1	$50,000
2	60,000	2	20,000
3	90,000	3	100,000
4	120,000	4	130,000
5	140,000	5	195,000

Roger was very pleased with Jennifer's suggestion and prepared to compute the returns. Just as he was beginning, Tai Ming, the Director of Foreign Operations, walked into the room and examined the new proposal.

Tai explained, "Foreign investments should not have a higher discount rate than domestic projects simply because they are riskier." He suggested that foreign investment brought diversity into the firm's portfolio of investments and actually reduced total corporate risk. He went so far as to suggest they might justify a 'lower discount rate.' As an example, he suggested that while the U.S. economy was in a recession in 2001-2002, many Asian economies were booming and investments there reduced risk.

Roger was appreciative of Tai's input but decided to run the numbers first based on current practices and Jennifer's suggestions and then further evaluate the merits of Tai's international diversification arguments.

Required

1. Compute the present value of the two investments in Figure 2 based on the current non risk-adjusted discount rate of 10 percent. Which of the two is superior?

2. Compute the present value of Investment A based on a risk-adjusted discount rate at 13 percent as applied to a new product in the domestic market.

3. Compute the present value of Investment B based on risk-adjusted discount rate of 17 percent as applied to introducing an established product in a foreign market.

4. Which of the two is superior under the risk-adjusted discount rate approach as utilized in questions two and three?

5. If the two projects were mutually exclusive, what would your decision be based on the analysis under the risk-adjusted discount rate approach?

6. If the two projects were non-mutually exclusive, and there was no capital rationing, what would your decision be based on the analysis under the risk-adjusted discount rate approach?

7. Do you agree with Tai Ming's arguments about the impact of international diversification on the discount rate? Note: there is no anticipated correct answer to this question. Please just give your opinion.

20

Inca, Inc.*

Inca, Inc., operated and licensed others to operate quick-service restaurants under the name Pedro's. The menu featured chiliburgers, along with a limited selection of Mexican foods. The walls of each restaurant were decorated with the exploits of Mexican heroes.

The first Pedro's was opened in Santa Fe, New Mexico, on June 9, 2000. Ten years later there were 298 restaurants in operation in 27 states, of which 111 were operated by the company and 187 by franchisees. In addition, 4 restaurants were under construction by the company, and 64 by franchisees. A balance sheet as of June 30, 2010, is included in Figure 1.

Each Pedro's restaurant was built to the same specifications for exterior style and interior décor. The buildings, constructed of yellow brick, were located on sites of approximately one acre. The parking lots, depending on the exact size and shape of the land, were designed for 30 to 35 cars. The standard restaurant contained about 1,900 square feet, seated 81 persons, and included a pickup window for drive-through service.

Locations were chosen in heavily populated areas, since success depend-ed upon serving a large number of customers.

All of the restaurants offered the same menu. Three sizes of chiliburgers were featured: the Gaucho (quarter pound), the Soldado (half pound), and the Matador (three-quarter pound). The names were integrated into the company's advertising. On television each commercial gave special attention to one of the three themes.

The prospective franchisee signed a document that included the option of operating a specified number of Pedro's restaurants in a prescribed geographical area. Each new location required an initial payment of $18,000. In addition, a royalty of 5 percent of gross sales was specified. It was also stipulated that franchisees must spend at least 2 percent of gross receipts on local advertising. Inca, Inc., believed that properly trained employees were the key to success. Therefore, managers and company trainees were

* From Henry R. Kuniansky and William H. Marsh, *Case Problems in Financial Management* (Englewood Cliffs, N.J.; Prentice-Hall).

required to attend a three-week program covering all aspects of company operations. More than 600 people were graduated from the school during 2009.

Inca, Inc., planned to begin construction on five new company – owned restaurants during 2011. The exact size of the buildings had not been determined, although the had not been determined, although the specific sites had already been selected.

Figure 1

INCA, INC.
Balance Sheet
As of June 30, 2010
(in thousands)

Assets

Current assets:
Cash	$12,026
Accounts receivable	1,646
Inventory	512
Other current assets	1,872
Total current assets	16,056

Equipment and property:
Buildings	10,208
Leasehold improvements	4,826
Restaurant equipment	11,630
Motor vehicles	1,188
Office equipment	464
Lease rights	542
Less: Accumulated depreciation	3,104
Total equipment and property	25,754
Land	10,606
Construction in progress	434
Other assets	1,566
Total assets	$54,416

Liabilities and Stockholders' Equity

Current liabilities:
Notes payable to banks	$ 316
Accounts payable	3,846
Income taxes	1,754
Accrued liabilities	1,314
Current portion, term debt	1,564
Total current liabilities	8,794
Long-term debt, less current portion	17,742

Deferred:
Income taxes	982
Franchise fees	3,730
	4,712

Stockholders' equity:
Common stock, $0.10 par	676
Capital in excess of stated value	9,726
Retained earnings	12,766
Total stockholders' equity	23,168
Total liabilities and stockholders' equity	$54,416

Figure 2

INCA, INC.
Present Value of Cash Flows
(in thousands)

Restaurant Size	Level of Demand		Outcomes (NPV)
Standard	High	(.40)	$1,050
	Medium	(.40)	630
	Low	(.20)	(200)
Expanded	High	(.40)	2,812
	Medium	(.40)	740
	Low	(.20)	(900)

Management believed that restaurants with a capacity of 144 persons would be more profitable than the present size of 81.

The company faced two choices: continuing with the smaller-size units or going to the larger size. The initial cost for five smaller restaurants was $2.1 million, and it was $3.7 million for five larger ones. Demand expectations over the years were 40 percent for high demand, 40 percent for medium demand, and 20 percent for low demand. The net present values of cash flows for the two proposals are given in Figure 2.

John H. Porter had been president and chief executive officer of Inca, Inc., since July of 2002. Prior to that time he had worked for a competitor. He knew the decision concerning the size of new restaurants could be a major turning point for the company. Mr. Porter wondered if the potential higher returns for the larger units justified the increased risk. In any event, the strategy would have to be sold to the board of directors.

Required

1. Determine the expected value of the net present value for the standard-size restaurants. Use the data in Figure 2. To get the expected value, multiply the outcomes (NPV) times the appropriate probability (.40 for high demand, etc.). Do this for high demand, medium demand, and low demand, and sum to answer this question. Remember to state your final answer in thousands.
2. Follow the same procedure for the expanded-size restaurants to arrive at the expected value of the net present value.
3. Which alternate appears to be the more desirable?
4. Next, determine the standard deviation for the standard size restaurants. Remember to state your final answer in thousands. The standard deviation for the expanded-size restaurant is $1,415,800.
5. Now determine the coefficient of variation for the two alternatives.

Required

6. Based on the coefficient of variation, which of the two alternatives is more desirable? Comment on the relationship of your answer to question 3 and your answer to this question. What general principle is being demonstrated?

7. Assume, in addition to considering the building of five restaurants that are all standard or all expanded, Inca evaluates possible combinations of the two. The following values will apply for the expected values and the standard deviations.

	Standard Deviation	Expected Value
4 standard, 1 expanded	$ 641,630	$ 753,760
3 standard, 2 expanded	832,460	875,420
2 standard, 3 expanded	1,025,800	997,280
1 standard, 4 expanded	1,220,400	1,119,040

If the firm wishes to minimize risk, which of the six alternatives should it choose? (Refer to your answer to question 5 as well as this question.)

CASE

21

Robert Boyle & Associates, Inc.

On a Saturday afternoon in May 2008, Robert Boyle and his wife Janet were sitting on the porch of their house on Nantucket Island, Massachusetts, watching the fog roll in. The couple frequently spent weekends on the island, when the demands of Robert's business and Janet's teaching job would permit. Robert was the president of Robert Boyle & Associates, a closely held real estate investment trust (REIT) located in Auburn, Massachusetts. From a small office there, Robert had been managing the development of shopping centers for a little over eight years. Robert conducted most of the business himself, and the "associates," a group of about 40 friends, family members, and business colleagues, provided most of the financing. The trust had been quite successful, and today it owned two shopping centers, which produced rental income of almost $6 million in 2007. (See Figures 1 and 2 for Boyle & Associates' financial statements for 2005.)

"You know, Janet," Bob said wistfully, "we ought to move out here permanently. There's just no comparison between life here and on the mainland."

"You get no argument from me," Janet replied. "I've been telling you that ever since we bought this house. You could develop real estate just as easily from here as in the city, you know. Which reminds me, what's the latest on the Nantucket Center project? You've been quiet about it for about a week now." Janet referred to a proposal Robert had made a few months ago to build the first shopping center on Nantucket Island.

Robert sighed. "Well, it's on the back burner right now for lack of financing. I'm convinced that it would make us a lot of money; but, the trouble is, it will take a lot of money to get it built—about $10 million, in fact, and that's more than we've ever had to raise before."

"Oh, come on," Janet said. (She had always been an active participant in the business.) "You've built two shopping centers, so far, and didn't have any trouble getting the money for them. Why don't you just borrow some more?"

"Too much borrowed already, I'm afraid," Robert replied. "Our debt-to-assets ratio is quite a bit over the average for REITs now, and our investment banker says that another loan, or even a bond issue, would be quite expensive in terms of interest cost." (See Figure 3 for comparisons between Boyle & Associates and a sample of other REITs.)

Figure 1

ROBERT BOYLE & ASSOCIATES, INC.
Income Statement
For the year 2007
(in millions)

Loan income	$0.240
Rental income	5.992
Other income	0.168
Total income	6.400
Depreciation	0.920
General and administrative expenses	0.435
Operating income	5.045
Interest expense	0.945
Net income	$4.100
Dividend paid	$3.915

Note: Boyle & Associates qualifies as a REIT so it pays no income tax.

Figure 2

ROBERT BOYLE & ASSOCIATES, INC.
Balance Sheet
As of December 31, 2007
(in millions)

Assets:	
Cash and equivalents	$ 2.100
Land development and construction loans	2.000
Property owned, net of depreciation	16.000
Other assets	0.900
Total assets	$21.000
Liabilities and equity:	
Bank borrowings	$ 2.000
Mortgages on property	7.000
Other liabilities	0.450
Total liabilities	9.450
Common stock (4 million shares, $1 par)	4.000
Additional paid-in capital	7.450
Retained earnings	0.100
Total equity	11.550
Total liabilities and equity	$21.000

"Well, what about the shareholders?" Janet insisted. "Can't they contribute some more equity money?" (Boyle & Associates' 40 existing stockholders held 4 million shares with a book value of $2.89 each.)

Robert responded with a smile. "You know the answer to that already," he said. "You and I are the biggest stockholders. But even if all 40 stockholders put in an equal amount it would cost each of us $250,000. You and I don't have that kind of cash, and I'm sure the rest of the stockholders don't, either."

"Well, then," Janet continued unperturbed, "you need some more stockholders. Why don't you sell stock to the public? I'm sure it would be a great success once people knew what the company's plans were."

"Yes, that's what our investment banker said, too," Robert replied. "But I have some reservations. For instance, look at the dilution effect. You know, to qualify as a REIT, and, therefore, to pay no income tax at the corporate level, we pay out 95 percent of earnings every year as dividends. Anything that affects earnings per share, then, affects the shareholders' dividends. If we issue a whole lot of new stock, earnings per share will be diluted severely, and the existing stockholders will be most unhappy!"

"But, Robert," Janet said, "aren't you ignoring the money you will make on the proceeds of the stock issue? It seems to me that the income from the investment ought to more than offset the initial dilution, producing even more earnings—and dividends—than before. Surely the stockholders will see that."

"Maybe so," Robert said, "but that's not the only problem. Suppose, for example, that the whole shopping center deal falls through?" (It was not certain at this time that the residents and government authorities on Nantucket would approve the project.) "If it does, the price of our company's shares, now publicly traded, will surely fall, to the dismay and embarrassment of us all. You know, managing a publicly traded company is not at all like managing a private one. The pressure for short-term performance is terrific. If I don't produce, I'll be voted out of office at the next shareholders' meeting."

"And that's another thing," Robert continued, warming up, "shareholders' meetings. Look what you have to go through as a publicly traded company: shareholders' meetings, annual reports, SEC filings, disclosure notices, regulators poking around; why, the administrative tasks alone will require a couple of full-time people! Besides that, look at the cost of the issue itself. The investment banker will take a cut of about 6.5 percent of the issue, and we'll have to pay about $60,000 out-of-pocket for legal and accounting fees and printing expenses. I bet we'd have to issue almost $11 million in stock just to get $10 million in cash. Pretty expensive!"

"Yes, that's so," Janet agreed. "But even so, the benefits might outweigh the costs. One thing you haven't mentioned is the increase in liquidity for the company's shares you would get if they were publicly traded. You know most of our existing shareholders have been with us for the whole eight years, and they have quite a bit of money tied up in this one basket. How can they diversify their portfolios or sell their holdings outright? I bet they'd love to see the shares publicly traded in the market with an established price."

"All right, you may have a point," Robert conceded. "Tell you what, I'll write a letter to our existing stockholders outlining the pros and cons, and ask them to respond with recommendations. If the prevailing sentiment is to go public, we'll do it, and if it's not, we won't. In the end, though, the whole discussion may depend on how badly we want to build the Nantucket Center. If we want it, we'll probably have to go public to build it."

"I knew you would have it all figured out," Janet said, approvingly. "Now, how about a martini?"

Figure 3
Industry data and
comparisons
(in millions)

Company	Total Revenue	Net Income	Number of Shares
JNB Realty Trust..	4.3	2.6	1.423
USP REIT	7.8	1.5	2.500
Cousins Properties, Inc.	52.5	29.6	17.165
Bradley REIT	7.1	1.3	3.360
Mortgage Growth Investors, Inc.	14.0	9.9	7.730
Dial REIT (newly established)	—	—	1.736
Average of companies listed	14.3	7.5	5.653
Robert Boyle & Associates	6.4	4.1	4.000

Company	Return on Equity	Return on Assets	Debt to Assets
JNB Realty Trust..	10.8%	9.6%	0.11
USP REIT	12.2	4.5	0.63
Cousins Properties, Inc.	26.7	23.7	0.11
Bradley REIT	19.2	7.3	0.62
Mortgage Growth Investors, Inc.	8.0	6.9	0.14
Dial REIT (newly established)	—	—	0.25
Average of companies listed	12.8	8.7	0.31
Robert Boyle & Associates	35.5	19.5	0.45

Long-Term Debt	Total Equity	Total Assets	Earnings Per Share	Dividend Per Share	Book Value Per Share
$3.1	$24.0	$27.1	$1.83	$1.75	$16.84
21.2	12.3	33.5	0.60	0.57	4.92
14.1	110.7	124.8	1.72	1.64	6.45
11.0	6.8	17.8	0.39	0.37	2.01
19.8	123.9	143.7	1.28	1.23	16.03
10.3	31.3	41.6	—	1.64	18.02
13.3	51.5	64.7	0.97	1.20	10.71
9.5	11.6	21.0	1.03	0.98	2.89

Asset Turnover	Net Profit* Margin	5-Year EPS Growth	Dividend yield	Price-Earnings Ratio	Recent Stock Price
0.16	60.5%	1.1%	11.7%	8.2	$15.00
0.23	19.2	8.1	5.8	16.3	9.75
0.42	56.4	2.9	9.8	9.7	16.75
0.40	18.3	12.3	2.8	34.2	13.25
0.10	70.9	7.1	6.2	15.5	19.88
—	—	—	8.5	—	19.25
0.22	37.5	5.3	7.5	14.0	$15.65
0.30	64.1	9.7			

* This figure tends to be high for REITs because of relatively low expenses relative to revenue.

Required

1. Refer to Figure 3 for comparisons between Boyle & Associates and other REITs. Note the industry average price–earnings ratio. The investment banker will set Boyle's P/E ratio based on how the company compares to the industry average in six areas: return on equity, return on assets, debt to assets, asset turnover, net profit margin, and five-year earnings per share growth. The investment banker will start with the industry average P/E, and will add one-half point for each of the areas in which Boyle is superior to the industry, and will subtract one-half point for each area in which Boyle is inferior to the industry. After tabulating the results, the investment banker will subtract one point for good measure to ensure the issue presents an attractive opportunity. On this basis, what will the banker determine to be the proper P/E ratio for Boyle & Associates?

2. Considering that the banker's spread will be 6.5 percent of the total issue size, and Boyle will have to pay $60,000 out-of-pocket expenses, what is the total issue size necessary to yield $10 million in cash to the company? Use the formula: $X - .065X - \$60,000 = \$10,000,000$. X is the issue size. Round your answer upward to the nearest $100,000.

3. Assume 699,029 shares will be sold at a public price of $15.45 to provide approximately $10.8 million. What dollar return on the net proceeds of the offering must Boyle & Associates earn to bring earnings per share up to what it was before the offering? ($1.03) After you compute the dollar return on the net proceeds, convert this to a ratio (percentage of net proceeds).

   Compare this answer to Boyle's return on assets in 2005 (Figure 3). Based on the company's performance in 2005, do you think the required return can be earned?

4. If half of Boyle's associates decide to sell their existing shares in addition to the initial offering, how many total shares will have to be issued by the company to yield $10 million in cash to the company?

5. Summarize the pros and cons of Boyle & Associates going public from the information in the case and your reading of the text, Chapter 15. If you were one of the existing stockholders and you received Robert Boyle's letter, would you recommend going public or not? What would be the major reason affecting your opinion?

Glazer Drug Company

Generic Drug Industry

Generic drugs are the equivalents of brand-name drugs, typically sold under their generic chemical names at prices below those of their brand-name equivalents. Generic drugs may be manufactured and marketed only if relevant patents on their brand-name equivalents have expired, been challenged or invalidated, or otherwise validly circumvented.

Future generic industry growth can be attributed to both a large number of branded drugs losing patent protection in the coming years and a strengthened desire by healthcare payers to increase generic drug utilization. The generic industry has seen rapid growth since the mid-80's. Accompanying this growth has been a growing desire within the industry to challenge the legality of branded drug patents in court, often enabling patents to be overturned years ahead of schedule. Also attributing to the rapid generic growth id the appeal of Healthcare payers, such as large employers like GM and pharmacy benefit managers (PBMs) like Medco Health Systems, to increasingly direct their clients to buy more and more generics.

The Going Public Transaction

Glazer Drug Co. is the fourth largest generic drug company in the world, with annual sales of over $3 billion. It trails only Norvatis AG, Teva Pharmaceutical, and Mylan Labs in sales and profits. Its home office is in St. Louis, with its laboratories and sales outlets in the U.S. and 30 foreign countries, with the largest foreign operations in Great Britain and Australia. Its generic brand labels cover medication for heart disease, diabetes, acute infections, and many other ailments.

In the fall of 2007, the company decided to go public. Its investment banker was Aaron, Barkley, and Company.

Glazer Drug Co.'s most recent 12 month earnings were $150 million with one hundred million shares, providing an EPS figure of $1.50. After conducting a careful analysis of the generic drug industry, the investment banker decided a P/E of 25 would be appropriate, giving the stock a value of

$37.50. Allowing for the underwriting speed, the net to the corporation and selling stockholders was $36.68. The out-of-pocket underwriting expense was $2 million on the 20 million chares that were to be sold to the public. Ten million of the 20 million shares in the IPO were new corporate shares and the remaining 10 million were shares currently owned by Larry Glazer, one of the founders of the company. The 10 million shares sold by Glazer represented 85 percent of his holdings.

On the day of the offering, the stock price shot up from $37.50 to $51.10 a share, and by January 1, 2008, the stock had reached a price of $61.75. Since no specific events involving the company had taken place, it appeared that the stock market had a favorable impression of the firm.

Required

1. What was the percent underwriting speed?
2. Subsequent to the issue, by what amount would earnings per share be diluted?
3. What are the net proceeds to the corporation from the issue?
4. What rate of return would the corporation need to earn on the net proceeds to avoid dilution? Note: because of the relatively high P/E of 25, the answer is less than 5 percent. However, the P/E does not figure directly into the calculation.
5. Using the original earnings per share of $1.50, what would the P/E ratio be based on the stock price of $61.75 on January 1, 2008?
6. Should Mr. Glazer be happy about the pricing of the stock by the investment banker and the movement of the stock price after the public offering?

23

Leland Industries

Leland Industries is the nation's fifth largest producer of bakery and snack goods, with operations primarily located in the southeastern United States. Over the last 10 years, Leland had been one of the most efficient bakeries in the nation, with a 10-year average sales growth of 9.8 percent and an average return on equity of 16.8 percent. Management goals for the company include 10 percent earnings growth per year, and an average return of 16.8 percent on equity over time.

Late in the year 2008, Leland reached an agreement with a major food chain to provide private label bakery service in addition to its own products that are sold to Krogers, Albertson's, and many other grocery stores. The new private label program had significant start-up costs, including new packaging techniques and the addition of 250 sales routes.

Al Oliver, the vice president of finance, believed in maintaining a balanced capital structure, and since a 1 million share stock issue totaling $25 million in value had been offered earlier in the year, he thought this was a good time to go to the debt market. Previously, the firm's debt issues had been privately placed with insurance

companies and pension funds, but Al believed this was an appropriate time to approach the public markets based on the company's recent strong performance.

He called his investment banker and was told that the rating that the firm received from Standard and Poor's and Moody's would be a key variable in determining the interest rate that would be paid on the debt issue. Leland industries intended to issue $20 million of new debt.

A comparison of Leland Industries to other bakeries is shown in Figure 1. The other five firms all had issued debt publicly according to Ben Gilbert, who was Leland Industries' major contact at the investment banking firm of Gilbert, Rollins and Ross.

As an alternative to a straight bond issue, Ben Gilbert suggested that the firm consider issuing floating rate or even zero-coupon rate bonds. He said the principal advantage to the floating rate bonds was that they could be issued at 1¼ percent below the going market rate for straight debt issues. Al Oliver was pleasantly surprised to hear this, and asked his investment banker what the catch was. Al had heard too many times that "there is no such thing as a free lunch." His investment banker explained that with a floating rate bond the problem of interest rate changes was shifted from the borrower to the lender. To quote Ben Gilbert:

Normally the risk of changes in yield to maturity is a burden or opportunity that bondholders must consider. If yields go up, bond prices of existing bonds go down and the opposite is true if rates decline. There is a risk and many investors do not like this risk. With a floating rate bond the interest rate that the investor directly receives changes with market conditions and therefore the bond tends to trade at its initial par value. For example, if a bond were issued at 9 percent interest for 20 years and market rates went to 13 percent, a floating rate bond would adjust its payment up to 13 percent, and the market value would remain at $1,000. On a straight bond issue the interest rate would remain at 9 percent and because it is 4 percent below the market, the bond price would drop to the $700 range.

Al Oliver quickly perceived that with a floating rate bond he could pay 1¼ percent lower interest than with a fixed rate bond, but that in future years he could not predict what his interest rates would be. He was pretty turned off by the whole idea until his investment banker suggested that the futures and options experts at Gilbert, Rollins and Ross could hedge this risk at a probable aftertax cost of about $120,000 per year. While he was making this point, Ben Gilbert gave Al Oliver a copy of *Foundations of Financial Management* by Block and Hirt and suggested that he review the material on hedging at the end of Chapter 8. Al Oliver knew that he must make a decision about the benefits and costs of floating rate bonds.

Before the discussion was over, Al Oliver was presented with one last option. It was possible the firm might wish to issue zero-coupon rate bonds. Because no interest was paid on an annual basis and the only gain to the investor came in the form of capital appreciation, Al Oliver initially liked the idea. However, he remembered the no free lunch argument and asked Ben Gilbert what drawbacks there might be to this type of issue. Ben responded:

Well, Al, since you are not paying annual interest or retiring any part of the issue during its life, there can be greater risk, which may mean there is a lower rating on the issue. You, of course, know what that means in terms of a higher required yield on the bond issue.

Al Oliver thought he would need to put some numbers to zero-coupon bonds as well as many of the other items that Ben Gilbert brought up. He called his young assistant in for some help.

Figure 1	Bond ratings of comparative firms

International Bakeries

Debt to total assets	30%	Bond price	$1,100
Times interest earned	7.1X	Annual interest	10.35%
Fixed charge coverage	5.0X	Maturity	25 years
Current ratio	3.1X	Par value	$1,000
Return on stockholders' equity	22%	(principal payment)	
Rating	AA1		

Gates Bakeries

Debt to total assets	42%	Bond price	$920
Times interest earned	5.5X	Annual interest	9.45%
Fixed charge coverage	4.2X	Maturity	20 years
Current ratio	2.3X	Par value	$1,000
Return on stockholders' equity	17.1%	(principal payment)	
Rating	A1		

Savanah Products

Debt to total assets	65%	Bond price	$1,150
Times interest earned	2.0X	Annual interest	15.75%
Fixed charge coverage	1.7X	Maturity	15 years
Current ratio	1.2X	Par value	$1,000
Return on stockholders' equity	7%	(principal payment)	
Rating	B3		

Dyer Pastries

Debt to total assets	35%	Bond price	$1,060
Times interest earned	6.0X	Annual interest	10.30%
Fixed charge coverage	3.6X	Maturity	20 years
Current ratio	2.8X	Par value	$1,000
Return on stockholders' equity	19%	(principal payment)	
Rating	AA3		

Nolan Bread

Debt to total assets	47%	Bond price	$950
Times interest earned	4.9X	Annual interest	10.30%
Fixed charge coverage	3.8X	Maturity	25 years
Current ratio	2.1X	Par value	$1,000
Return on stockholders' equity	15%	(principal payment)	
Rating	A2		

Leland Industries*

Debt to total assets	44%
Times interest earned	5.7X
Fixed charge coverage	3.7X
Current ratio	2.0X
Return on stockholders' equity	16.8%
Rating: To be determined	

*
The first three ratios for Leland industries assume the impact of the new bond issue. Of course, these are approximations.
The bond rating agencies require such information.

Required

1. Based on the data in Figure 1, which rating do you think is most likely for Leland Industries?
2. Compute the approximate yield to maturity for the bonds of International Bakeries, Gates Bakeries, and Savanah Products.
3. What is the percentage aftertax cost of debt for the bond issues listed in question 2? Refer to Chapter 11 for the aftertax cost of debt formula. Assume a tax rate of 35 percent for the three firms.
4. If the bonds of Leland Industries carried a requirement that 5 percent of the bonds outstanding be retired each year, what would be the total amount of bonds outstanding after the third year? Based on an assumed 10 percent annual interest rate for Leland, which is consistent with the comparable companies, and a tax rate of 35 percent, what would be the aftertax dollar cost of interest payments on this sum?
5. From a strictly dollars and cents viewpoint, does the floating rate bond with the hedging approach appear to be viable? Base your analysis on the new $20 million of debt outstanding, the 1¼ percent interest savings, and after-tax dollars.
6. Assume the zero-coupon rate bonds would be issued at 11 percent for 20 years, what will be the initial price of a $1,000 bond? Use Appendix B to find the present value (price of the bond). How many bonds must be issued to raise $20 million? What is the danger in issuing the zero-coupon rate bonds?

Warner Motor Oil Company

Gina Thomas was concerned about the effect that high interest expenses were having on the bottom line reported profits of Warner Motor Oil Co. Since joining the company three years ago as vice president of finance, she noticed that operating profits appeared to be improving each year, but that earnings after interest and taxes were declining because of high interest charges.

Because interest rates had finally started declining after a steady increase, she thought it was time to consider the possibility of refunding a bond issue. As she explained to her boss, Al Rosen, refunding meant calling in a bond that had been issued at a high interest rate and replacing it with a new bond that was similar in most respects, but carried a lower interest rate. Bond refunding was only feasible in a period of declining interest rates. Al Rosen, who had been the CEO of the company for the last seven years understood the general concept, but he still had some questions.

He said to Gina, "If interest rates are going down, bond prices are certain to be going up. Won't that make it quite expensive to buy outstanding issues so that we can replace them with new issues?" Gina had a quick and direct answer. "No, and the reason is that the old issues have a call provision associated with them." A call provision allows the firm to call in bonds at slightly over par (usually 8 to 10 percent above par) regardless of what the market price is.

The Proposed Refunding Decision

Gina thought if she could present a specific example to Al he would have a better feel for the bond refunding process. She proposed to call in an 11.50 percent $30,000,000 issue that was scheduled to mature in the year 2025. The bonds had been issued in 2005 and since it was now 2010, the bonds had 15 years remaining to maturity. It was Gina's intent to replace the bonds with a new $30,000,000 issue that would have the same maturity date 15 years into the future as that of the original 2005 issue. Based on advice from the firm's investment banking firm, Walston and Sons, the bonds could be issued at a rate of 10 percent. Joe Walston, a senior partner in the investment banking firm, further indicated that the underwriting cost on the new issue would be 2.8 percent of the $30,000,000 amount involved.

Before she could do her analysis, Gina needed to accumulate information on the old 11.50 percent bond issue that she was proposing to refund. The original bond indenture indicated that the bonds had an 8 percent call premium, and that the bonds could be called anytime after five years. Gina explained to Al Rosen that the bondholders were protected from having their bonds called in for the first five years after issue, but that the bonds were fair game after that. Furthermore, from the sixth through the 13th year, the call premium went down by 1 percent per year. By the 14th year after issue, there was no call premium and the corporation could merely call in the bonds at par. Since in this case five years had passed, the call premium would be exactly eight percent.

Gina knew that the underwriting cost on the old issue was important to the calculations related to the refunding decision. She checked with the chief accountant and found out they had initially been $400,000.

The firm was currently paying taxes at a rate of 30 percent and would use a discount rate of 7 percent for bond refunding decisions.

Required

1. Before you do the bond refunding analysis, determine what the current price of the old bonds would be for the previously issued bonds in the marketplace. Do the example based on a $1,000 bond using semiannual analysis. As specified in the case, the bonds have 15 years remaining. The interest rate at the time of issue was 11.50 percent, but is now 10 percent.

2. As a result of paying the 8 percent call premium over par instead of the market price determined in question 1, how much will the firm save on each old $1,000 bond in reacquiring it?

3. Using the four steps outlined in Chapter 16 of the text for a bond refunding decision, determine whether the potential refunding has a positive net present value. (Round all values to the nearest dollar).

4. Assuming you did your calculations correctly in question 3, you should have gotten a positive net present value. If not, you will want to rerun your numbers. Now assume Gina goes to Al Rosen with these numbers and suggests they do the refunding because there is a positive net present value. What is an additional important consideration that Gina and Al must consider before they go ahead with the refunding and all the associated costs?

5. Assume that before Warner Motor Oil Company can get the refunding completed, interest rates on new 15 year bonds goes up to 10.4 percent. Assume all other numbers previously given are the same, should the refunding be undertaken?

Midsouth Exploration Company

Lou Matson, President of Midsouth Exploration Company, knew that circumstances had finally become favorable for drilling for oil in March of 2006. For the last three years conditions had been miserable for oil companies. As the price of oil slipped to $10 a barrel, it was no longer economically feasible to search for new sources of petroleum. However, the booming world economy in the first quarter of 2008, along with restricted output by OPEC and other oil-producing nations, had sent the price of oil to over $30 a barrel.

Midsouth Exploration had extensive holdings in Louisiana and East Texas that had largely gone unattended over the last three years. When Lou Matson called his chief geologist, Harold Boudreaux, the drilling expert quickly informed Matson that all systems were go from an exploration viewpoint.

Raising Capital

However, Midsouth had a problem and that was raising capital to carry out the new exploration. While the firm often formed limited partnerships for specific projects, permanent capital was also required to support the increased operations of the firm. A recent conversation with Arthur Barnes III, the managing director of the investment-banking firm of Barnes, Colson, and Wilson, Inc., lead Mr. Matson to believe that immediate and decisive financing activity was necessary.

Thirty million dollars in new capital needed to be raised as a base for future operations. Because of the risky nature of the firm's business, debt financing was out of the question. The investment banker suggested a new common stock issue might be the best alternative, but he also pointed out there was a potential problem.

In 1997, the company had issued $8.50 (dividend) cumulative preferred stock at $100 par value. There were 200,000 shares issued. The company promptly made payments on the preferred stock from 1999 to 2004. However, in the second half of 2005 and in 2006 and 2007 no preferred stock dividends were paid. Mr. Barnes, the investment banker, pointed out that common stock would be difficult to sell with the preferred stock dividend in arrears (unpaid). With cumulative preferred stock, no dividends can be paid to common stockholders unless all prior dividend claims by preferred stockholders have been satisfied. Of course, current claims must also be met.

Financing Plan

Mr. Barnes' investment banking experience led him to believe that any new common stock that Midsouth Exploration Company issued must pay dividends.

He suggested that if Midsouth sold common stock at $25 per share to the public (less $1.20 in flotation costs to the corporation), a $.50 per share common stock dividend would likely be necessary to attract investors.

Mr. Barnes further suggested that instead of attempting to pay all of the preferred stock dividends in arrears, the company offer the old preferred stockholders new preferred stock that is worth 50 percent more than the outstanding preferred stock (which is currently selling for the amount it is totally in arrears). The new preferred stock would pay a 9.2 percent dividend yield.

Because the old preferred stockholders would become new preferred stockholders, they would once again become dividend recipients, and would have a tax obligation related to the annual dividend yield of 9.2 percent.

Cost of Funding

As president of Midsouth Exploration Company, Mr. Matson liked the idea of exchanging new preferred stock for old preferred stock as well as selling new common stock. He was definitely willing to go along with the plan. However, there was one question that bothered him. Being a petroleum engineer, he had no formal business training and that, perhaps, was the reason behind his concern. He wondered why the firm had to pay a 9.2 percent dividend yield on preferred and only a 2 percent dividend yield on common stock ($.50 dividend/$25 stock price). His investment banker explained that the cost of common stock was not simply the cost of the dividend, but the total expected return to stockholders that must be earned to keep them satisfied. He suggested that investors in Midsouth Exploration Company had an expectation that the company would be able to grow at a 9.75 percent rate (g) in the future.

Required

1. Has the company broken any laws or agreements by failing to make dividend payments on the preferred stock?

2. How far is the company in arrears (behind) in its preferred stock dividends on a per share basis? How much is it totally in arrears on all shares?

3. What would be the price per share of the new preferred stock? How much would the new preferred stock's dividend per share be with a 9.2 percent yield?

4. Taking the 9.2 percent annual dividend rate, and assuming a 35 percent marginal tax rate for corporate investors, what would the percentage aftertax yield be on preferred stock for corporate investors? Recall that 70 percent of the preferred stock dividend is tax exempt to corporate investors and only 30 percent is taxable.

5. Compare the <u>cost</u> of new preferred stock to the <u>cost</u> of new common stock for the issuing corporation. (See Chapter 11 for formulas). There is no flotation cost on new preferred stock in this case since it is merely being exchanged for old preferred stock.

   Are there any tax benefits for the <u>issuing</u> corporation with either security?

6. Under the proposed financing plan to raise $30 million in new funds, how many new shares of common stock must be issued? The out-of-pocket costs will be $250,000, while the underwriting spread (flotation cost) is $1.20.

26

Alpha Biogenetics

Alpha Biogenetics was founded in 1996 by Steve Menger, Ph.D., M.D. At the time, the company consisted of little more than a one room laboratory, Dr. Menger, and a lab assistant. However, Dr. Menger's outstanding research attracted the attention of the Scientific Venture Capital Fund and by 2003, the venture capital fund had contributed $4 million in so called "risk capital" funding. The financial support of the fund along with the work of Dr. Menger and other scientists who joined the company allowed Alpha Biogenetics to develop potential leading edge drugs in the areas of growth hormones, microgenes, and glycosylation inhibitors.

Future Development

In the year 2005, the company achieved its first profit of $1,600,000 and made a public offering of two million new shares at a price of $9.60 per share. At the same time, the Scientific Venture Capital Fund sold the 1.2M shares it had received for its capital contributions also at $9.60 per share. In the parlance of investment banking, the venture capitalist "cashed in its position".

Between the two million new shares sold by the firm and the 1.2 million old shares sold by the venture capitalist, 3.2 million shares were put in the hands of the public. At the same time, Dr. Menger held one million shares, three other Ph.D.'s working for the company had 600,000 shares in total and Ami Barnes, the chief financial officer, owned 200,000 shares. Altogether the insiders owned 1.8 million shares or 36 per-cent of the total of 5 million shares out-standing.

Outside shares	3.2 million	(64%)
Insider shares	1.8 million	(36%)
Shares outstanding	5.0 million	(100%)

By 2008, total earnings had increased to $4,800,000, and the stock price was $33.60. Also, many of the firm's products were well received in the biotech community.

However, there was one problem that troubled Dr. Menger and the other inside investors. They only had control of a minority interest of 36 percent of the shares outstanding. If an unfriendly takeover offer were to be made, they could be voted out of control of the company. While in the early stages of the development of the company, this was an unlikely event, such was no longer the case. The company now had products that others in the biotech industry such as Biogen, Cygnus, and Genetech might wish to acquire through a takeover. Most of these firms had their own high quality scientists that could quickly relate to the products being developed by Dr. Menger and Alpha Biogenetics.

Dr. Menger was particularly concerned because the year 2009 was not likely to be as good as prior ones and could make the company's stockholders a little less happy with its performance. Management was about to settle a lawsuit against the firm that could have adverse consequences in the year 2009. Also, the firm intended to replace its computer system and certain write-offs related to this were inevitable in the year 2009.

Dr. Menger expressed his concern to Bill Larson, who was a partner in the investment banking firm of Caruthers, Larson, and Rosen. Larson had been heavily involved in the initial public offering in 2005 of Alpha Biogenetics when his firm was the lead underwriter.

In response to Dr. Menger's concerns about an unfriendly takeover, Larson suggested the possibility of a poison pill. He said that poison pill provisions were used by over half the public corporations in the U.S. to thwart potentially unfriendly takeovers.

Poison pills could take many different forms, but Larson suggested that controlling inside stockholders be allowed to purchase up to 1,500,000 new shares in the firm at 70 percent of current market value if an outside group acquired 25 percent or more of the current shares outstanding. This provision could discourage a potential takeover offer as we shall see. Furthermore, Larson explained that poison pills do not require the approval of shareholders to implement as is true of other forms of anti-takeover amendments.

Annual Meeting

At the firm's 2008 annual meeting, Dr. Menger discussed the firm's financial performance for 2008 as well as seven other items on the agenda, including the election of members of the board of directors, the approval of the firm's auditors from Deloitte & Touche, LLP, and the announcement of the poison pill provision that the firm planned to implement in the next two months.

Dr. Menger was somewhat surprised at the strong reaction that he got on the latter item. An institutional stockholder that represented the California Public Employees Retirement System (CALPERS) said her multibillion dollar pension fund was really turned off by poison pill provisions, and that other large institutional investors felt the same way. She said that the role of corporate management was to maximize stockholder wealth and those anti-takeover provisions, such as poison pills, tended to discourage tender offers to purchase firms at premiums over current market value.

She further stated that poison pills tended to protect current management against the threat of being displaced and therefore gave them a feeling of security that sometimes lead to poor decisions, encouraged unusually high compensation packages, and even potential laziness.

There was a hush in the room after she finished her remarks. Dr. Menger felt compelled to answer her charges and stated that the poison pill provision was not intended to protect poor performance, but was being put into place to provide a sense of permanency to the current management. He said that if management became overly concerned with job security and short-term quarter to quarter performance, they would not take a long-term perspective that was essential to building a company for the future. As an example, he suggested that R & D expenditures might be cut back to beef up a quarterly earnings report.

He also said that a sense of security and permanency allowed the company to compete for top notch scientists and managers who otherwise would be hesitant to give up their current positions to go to a company that was a takeover target.

Bill Larson, the firm's investment banker, also got into the discussion. He said that while in certain instances poison pills thwarted potential stockholder value maximizing offers; in other cases it had the opposite effect. Because the company was protected against capricious or minimal takeover offers, companies that wanted to acquire firms with poison pill provisions tended to offer a premium price well above the average offer. This was necessary because the firm could easily deflect a normal offer.

As Dr. Menger took all these comments in, he decided to have one last meeting with his executive committee on the topic of implementing a poison pill provision.

Required

1. What were the earnings per share and the P/E ratio in the year that the firm went public (2005)?
2. Assuming a five percent underwriting spread, and $120,000 in out-of-pocket costs, what were the net proceeds to the corporation?
3. What rate of return did the Scientific Venture Capital Fund earn on its $4 million investment? Does this appear to be reasonable?
4. What were earnings per share in 2008? Based on the stock price of $33.60, what was the P/E ratio?
5. Under the poison pill provision, how much would it cost an unfriendly outside party to acquire 25 percent of the shares outstanding at the 2008 stock price?
6. Now assume an unfriendly, outside party acquired all the shares not owned by the inside control group:
    How many shares must the inside control group buy from the corporation to maintain its majority position? What would the total dollar cost be?
7. Based on the pro and con arguments made at the annual meeting, do you think that poison pills are in the best interest of stockholders? Please give your opinion on this because there is no one correct answer.

27

Montgomery Corporation

In January 2006, the board of directors of Montgomery Corporation, one of the nation's largest retail store chains, was having its regularly scheduled meeting to establish and declare the next quarterly dividend. (Statements for the firm and industry are shown in Figures 1 and 2.) However, this meeting wasn't so regular. One of the directors, Sidney Mobler, who was also a vice president in the company and chief financial officer, had brought a guest: Don Jackson, a financial analyst. Don had spent a considerable amount of time in the finance department and more than a few hours in Mr. Mobler's office developing a proposal concerning the company's dividend policy. He had finally convinced Mr. Mobler to allow him to present his idea to the board.

"Ladies and gentlemen," Don began, after being introduced by Mr. Mobler, "I'll skip the preliminaries and get right to the point. I think that Montgomery's dividend policy is not in the best interest of the stockholders."

Observing the rather chilly stares from around the room, he hastened on: "Now, I don't mean we have a bad policy, or anything like that; it's just that I think we could do an even better job of increasing our stockholders' wealth with a few small changes." He paused for effect. "Let me explain. Up to now our policy has been to pay a constant dividend every year, while increasing it occasionally to reflect the company's growth in sales and income. The problem is, that policy takes no account of the investment opportunities that the company has from year to year. In other words, this year we will use most of our net income to pay the same, or a greater, dividend than last year, even though there might be company investments available that would pay a much greater return if we committed the funds to the firm's investments instead. In effect, the stockholders are being shortchanged: They will realize perhaps a 6 percent yield on their investment as a result of receiving the dividend, when they could realize a 12 percent or higher return as a result of the company's return on its investments. I see this as a serious shortcoming in the management of the stockholders' funds.

"Now, fortunately, correcting this situation is not difficult. All you have to do is adopt what is called a *residual* dividend policy. That is, each year the firm would allocate money from income to those capital spending projects for which the return—that is, IRR—is greater than the cost of capital. Any money that is not used in the capital budget would be paid out to the stockholders in the form of dividends. In this way the firm would ensure that the stockholders' money is working the hardest way it can for them."

Figure 1

Selected financial data, Montgomery Corporation (in millions, except per share data)

	1999	2000	2001	2002	2003	2004	2005
Sales...............................	$27,357.4	$30,019.8	$35,882.9	$38,828.0	$40,715.3	$44,281.5	$48,000.0
Net income......................	$ 650.1	$ 861.2	$ 1,342.2	$ 1,454.8	$ 1,303.3	$ 1,351.3	$ 1,700.0
Amount to preferred dividends........	—	—	—	$ 16.7	$ 21.5	$ 16.8	$ 22.6
Amount to common dividends.........	$ 429.1	$ 476.3	$ 537.0	$ 630.8	$ 639.0	$ 648.3	$ 725.4
Amount to retained earnings.........	$ 221.0	$ 384.9	$ 805.2	$ 807.3	$ 642.8	$ 686.2	$ 952.0
Common shares outstanding........	347.9	351.4	354.6	361.6	363.1	376.6	378.0
Earnings per share (on average common shares)............	$ 1.96	$ 2.46	$ 3.80	$ 4.06	$ 3.60	$ 3.65	$ 4.51
DPS (on average common shares)........	$ 1.36	$ 1.36	$ 1.48	$ 1.70	$ 1.76	$ 1.76	$ 1.96
Payout ratio (DPS/EPS)*........	69.4%	55.3%	38.9%	41.8%	48.9%	48.2%	43.5%
Total retained earnings..........	$ 7,041.2	$ 7,426.1	$ 8,231.3	$ 9,038.6	$ 9,681.4	$10,367.6	$11,319.6
Cash balance....................	$ 1,170.7	$ 1,307.6	$ 1,502.5	$ 1,765.0	$ 2,357.2	$ 2,984.4	$ 3,235.0

*DPS (dividends per share)/EPS (earnings per share)

Figure 2   **Selected financial data, other retail chains**

	1999	2000	2001	2002	2003	2004	2005
Dillard Department Store:							
EPS	$0.69	$0.93	$1.38	$1.82	$2.29	$2.35	$2.50
DPS	$0.05	$0.05	$0.08	$0.09	$0.10	$0.12	$0.13
Payout ratio	7.3%	5.4%	5.8%	5.0%	4.4%	5.1%	5.2%
Dollar General:							
EPS	$0.38	$0.61	$0.81	$1.10	$0.95	$0.23	$0.30
DPS	$0.09	$0.11	$0.13	$0.17	$0.20	$0.20	$0.20
Payout ratio	23.7%	18.0%	16.1%	15.5%	21.1%	87.0%	66.7%
Limited, Inc.:							
EPS	$0.10	$0.19	$0.37	$0.51	$0.80	$1.21	$1.40
DPS	$0.01	$0.02	$0.04	$0.08	$0.11	$0.16	$0.24
Payout ratio	10.0%	10.5%	10.8%	15.7%	13.8%	13.2%	17.1%
Nordstrom, Inc.:							
EPS	$0.35	$0.38	$0.54	$0.55	$0.66	$0.91	$1.10
DPS	$0.06	$0.06	$0.07	$0.10	$0.11	$0.13	$0.18
Payout ratio	17.1%	15.8%	13.0%	18.2%	16.7%	14.3%	16.4%
J.C. Penney:							
EPS	$2.75	$2.94	$3.13	$2.91	$2.66	$3.53	$4.70
DPS	$0.92	$1.00	$1.08	$1.18	$1.18	$1.24	$1.48
Payout ratio	33.5%	34.0%	34.5%	40.6%	44.4%	35.1%	31.5%
Wal-Mart Stores:							
EPS	$0.16	$0.23	$0.35	$0.48	$0.58	$0.80	$1.10
DPS	$0.02	$0.02	$0.04	$0.05	$0.07	$0.09	$0.12
Payout ratio	12.5%	8.7%	11.4%	10.4%	12.1%	11.3%	10.9%

Note: DPS refers to dividends per share, EPS to earnings per share.

Mr. Clarence Autry, who was also on the board of directors of the Exxon corporation and no stranger to the world of corporate finance, broke in. "Young man," he said dryly, "your proposal ignores reality. It's not whether the stockholders are theoretically better off that counts, it's what they want. You cannot tell the stockholders you're doing what's best for them by cutting the dividend; the dividend is what they want. Not only is that dividend sure money in their pockets now, but the fact that it's the same size as last time, or even higher, is a signal to them that their company is doing well and will continue to do so in the future. These decisions can't always be made on the basis of good-looking formulas from the back room, you know."

Ms. Barbara Reynolds, who was the head of directors' auditing committee, and somewhat of an accounting expert, agreed with Mr. Autry. "That's a good point, Clarence, and one that's well recognized by our competitors, too. If you check, I don't think you'll find a single one of them that's cut their dividend in the last six years, even though their net income may have declined significantly. Furthermore, the whole argument is meaningless, anyway, because the dividend is not really competing with the capital budget for funds—we don't turn away profitable projects in favor of paying the dividend. If there are worthy projects in which we want to invest, and we would rather use our available cash to pay the dividend, then we seek financing for the investments from outside sources. In a way, we can have our cake and eat it too." She chuckled, pleased at the analogy.

Don Jackson, however, was not to be intimidated so easily. "Yes, ma'am, what you say is true," he replied, "and I would respond that competitors are not treating their stockholders fairly, either. Furthermore, you do seek outside financing occasionally for large projects, but there are two problems associated with doing it routinely, as you suggest. First, it might be viewed as borrowing, or issuing stock, to pay the dividend, which would cast the company in a very poor light. Second, it's more expensive to finance from outside sources than from inside due to the fees charged by the investment banker. Therefore, I believe you should exhaust our inside sources of financing before turning to the outside."

Ms. Reynolds held her ground. "That's all very well, but it's still not necessary to cut the dividend in order to fund the capital budget. As a last resort, if the company's cash balances were about to be drawn down too low, we could always declare a stock dividend instead of a cash dividend."

"Ladies, gentlemen, "Mr. Edward Asking, the chairman, intervened, "your comments are all very perceptive, but we must move on to the business at hand. All those in favor of changing to a residual policy, please raise your hand."

Required 1. *a.* Refer to Figure 1. Would you say that Montgomery's policy up to now has been to pay a constant dividend, with occasional increases as the company grows?

         b. Refer to Figure 2. What type of dividend policies would you say are being practiced by Montgomery's competitors in the retailing industry? Do you think that any firms are following a residual policy?

    2. *a.* Calculate the expected return to the common stockholders under the firm's present policy, given an expected dividend next year of $2.10 and a growth rate of 7.1 percent. Montgomery's stock currently sells for $35.

        (Use the dividend growth model):

$$\text{Expected return }(K_e) = \frac{D_1}{P_0} + g$$

        b. Assume that, if Don Jackson's proposal were adopted, next year's dividend would be zero but earnings growth would rise to 14 percent. What will be the expected return to the stockholders (assuming the other factors are held constant)?

    3. Is the size of the capital budget limited by the amount of net income, as Don implies? What is the maximum size that the capital budget can be in 2006 without selling assets or seeking outside financing?

    4. *a.* Don says the cost of the outside financing is more expensive than the cost of internal financing, due to the flotation costs charged by investment bankers. Given the data you have, what would you say is the firm's cost of internal equity financing?

        b. Assume Montgomery can sell bonds priced to yield 13 percent. What is the firm's aftertax cost of debt? (The tax rate is 25 percent.)

        c. Given the cost of debt and the cost of internal equity financing, why doesn't Montgomery just borrow the total amount needed to fund the capital budget and the dividend as well?

    5. Do you go along with Clarence Autry's comment that it's what the stockholders want that counts, not their total rate of return? Why or why not?

    6. Barbara Reynolds suggests that, if cash is needed for the capital budget, a stock dividend could be substituted for the cash dividend. Do you agree? How do you think the stockholders would react? Regardless of their reaction, is the stock dividend an equivalent substitute for the cash dividend?

    7. After all is said and done, do you think the firm's dividend policy matters? If so, what do you think Montgomery's policy should be?

28

Orbit Chemical Company

Orbit Chemical Co., located in Northbrook, Illinois, manufactures basic chemicals such as ethylene, vinyl chloride, and propylene. Although it is approximately 10 percent the size of its major competitors such as Du Pont, Dow Chemical, Monsanto, and Union Carbide, it still maintains a competitive position in the marketplace.

Robert Osborne, the CEO, had aggressively brought new products to the marketplace. These activities necessitated heavy new investment in plant and equipment. At the same time, Osborne thought it necessary to reduce the firm's amount of debt financing to present a better picture to the investment community. Net income had been increasing at a rate of five to 10 per year in the past few years and was expected to do so in the future. However, Osborne was upset that the stock was only trading at a P/E ratio of 7 times 2010 earnings per share.

As Osborne was beginning the process of financial planning for 2011, he received an E-mail message from Dan Morgan, the firm's vice president of finance. The message said, "Robert—I'm concerned about the dividend payment for 2011. Can we get together for a discussion at lunch on Tuesday?" Dan Morgan had recently been hired away from Logan Chemical Co. where he served as assistant corporate controller for two years and senior vice president for long-term planning for the three most recent years. Dan had a bachelor's degree in finance from the University of Maryland.

CEO Robert Osborne's initial strength had been in the laboratory. He received a Ph.D. in chemistry from the University of California at Berkeley 20 years ago. He began his career as a lab assistant at Eaton Chemical Corp. in Richmond, Virginia. As he progressed through the corporate ranks, he began to develop business skills and attended summer executive programs at the University of Virginia and Northwestern University. He eventually rose to the rank of executive vice president of Eaton Chemical Corp. When an executive recruiter contacted him about an open CEO position at Orbit Chemical Co., he decided to listen. He accepted a job offer at $500,000 a year (double his previous salary) and also received 200,000 stock options at an exercise price of $5 per share.

The Luncheon Meeting

At the luncheon meeting, Dan brought along the financial statements for year-end 2010. Figure 1 is the income statement, Figure 2, the balance sheet; and Figure 3, the statement of cash flows.

Dan was quick to point out that in spite of a profit of $106 million as shown in Figure 1, cash and marketable securities were only at $35 million in total as presented in Figure 2. Furthermore, there was a net decrease in cash and marketable securities of $59 million in 2010 as shown near the bottom of Figure 3. He once again emphasized a change in dividend policy might be necessary in 2011 due to cash flow considerations. Beth Ewing, a financial analyst at Orbit Chemical Co. who also joined the meeting, thought Dan made some good points, but also might be missing other important considerations related to financial analysis.

Figure 1

ORBIT CHEMICAL COMPANY
Income Statement
For the Year Ended December 31, 2010
(in thousands)

Sales	$942,000
Cost of goods sold	490,000
Gross profitt	452,000
Selling and administrative expense	104,000
Depreciation expense	60,000
Operating profit	288,000
Interest expense	126,000
Earnings before taxes	$162,000
Taxes	56,000
Earnings after taxes	106,000
Shares outstanding	100,000
Earnings per share	$1.06
Other information:	
Total dividends	$ 65,000
Dividends per share	$.65

Figure 2

ORBIT CHEMICAL COMPANY
Statement of Financial Position (Balance Sheet)
December 31, 2010
(in thousands)

Assets

Current assets:

Cash	$ 5,000
Marketable securities	30,000
Accounts receivable	155,000
Inventory	190,000
Total current assets..	$380,000

Other Assets:

Investments (long-term securities)	30,000

Fixed Assets:

Plant and equipment, original cost	$790,000	
Less: Accumulated depreciation	330,000	
Net plant and equipment		460,000
Total assets..		$870,000

Liabilities and Stockholders' Equity

Current liabilities:

Accounts payable	$130,000
Wages payable	15,000
Accrued expenses..	25,000
Total current liabilities	$170,000

Long-term liabilities:

Bonds payable, 2019 (reduced by $120,000 during 2006)	200,000
Total liabilities	$370,000

Stockholders' equity:

Common stock, $1 par value, 100,000 shares	100,000
Capital in excess of par	110,000
Retained earnings..	290,000
Total stockholders' equity......................................	$500,000
Total liabilities and stockholders' equity	$870,000

Figure 3

ORBIT CHEMICAL COMPANY
Statement of Cash Flows
For the Year Ended December 31, 2010
(in thousands)

Cash flows from operating activities:		
Net income (Earnings after taxes)		$106,000
Adjustments to determine cash flow from operating activities:		
Add back depreciation..	$ 60,000	
Increase in accounts receivable	(10,000)	
Decrease in inventory...	20,000	
Decrease in accounts payable..	(15,000)	
Increase in wages payable	5,000	
Increase in accrued expense	15,000	
Total adjustments		75,000
Net cash flows from operating activities..............................		$181,000
Cash flows from investing activities:		
Increase in investments (long-term securities).........................	(5,000)	
Increase in plant and equipment..	(50,000)	
Net cash flows from investing activities		($ 55,000)
Cash flows from financing activities:		
Decrease in bonds payable, retired part of debt due in 2019.....	($120,000)	
Common stock dividends paid	($ 65,000)	
Net cash flow from financing activities................................		($185,000)
Net increase (decrease) in cash flows		($ 59,000)
Cash and marketable securities (beginning of year)		$ 94,000
Cash and marketable securities (end of year)		$ 35,000

Required

1. Based on the information presented in Figures 1, 2, and 3, do you think that a change in the dividend policy will be necessary in 2011?

2. Regardless of your answer to question 1, assume that the firm has $30 million in funds that it is considering using for the repurchase of shares in the marketplace. The firm is currently trading at a low P/E ratio of 7 times 2010 earnings of $1.06 per share. The shares will be purchased in the open market and no premium will be paid over current price (as is sometimes the case). How many shares will be repurchased? (Round the final answer to the nearest whole number).

3. With the number of shares repurchased, what will be the recomputed value for 2010 earnings per share? (Round to two places to the right of the decimal point).

4. Assume the increased demand for the stock as a result of the share repurchase drives the P/E ratio up to 10, what will be the new stock price based on the earnings per share you computed in question 3?

5. Assume that Robert Osborne decides to use 50,000 of his stock options to purchase shares of common stock and he resells them in the market at the price you computed in question 4. What will his total before tax gain be?

6. What do you think the stock market's reaction will be to Robert Osborne exercising 50,000 of his options?

Hamilton Products

Andre Weatherby, an aspiring artist, had just sold his fifth painting of the year and now had $5,000 in cash to invest. His first inclination was to place his money in a federally insured savings and loan, but was disappointed to find out that his annual return would be less than five percent.

Knowing little about investment alternatives, he knew he must seek advice from a pro. He recalled that at his 10-year high school reunion he had run into Carol Upshaw, a University of Southern California finance major, who was now a stockbroker with Merrill Lynch.

Early Monday morning he called Carol and she said she would be able to provide Andre with help. During the course of their conversation, Andre indicated that he wanted to invest his funds in a stock or bond that provided a good annual return and also had the potential to increase in value. Beyond that, he was able to stipulate little else.

Carol considered a number of alternatives, but decided on Hamilton Products. She was particularly interested in the firm's convertible securities which paid 6.5 percent annual interest, and were also convertible into 27 shares of common stock. The bonds had a maturity date 20 years in the future. She explained to Andre that not only would he receive a good annual return, but could enjoy appreciation in value if the common stock did well.

The bonds were to be issued at a par value of $1,000 on the day that Andre called. The common stock of Hamilton Products was currently selling for $32.75 per share. Straight, non-convertible bonds of equal risk and maturity to those of Hamilton Products were currently yielding 8 percent. Carol said that because the bonds paid 6 ½ percent interest, they should hold up well in value even if the stock did poorly. The initial pure bond price value was $853.17.

Prospects for the Firm

Hamilton Products produced hot asphalt and ready mixed concrete and was located in California. The Transportant Act passed by Congress in late 1995 provided California with $12 billion dollars for highway and mass transit projects over the next six years. California already had matching funds from a special use tax now in place. Although the design and approval of new projects was taking longer than expected, by late 2007 competitive bidding on projects was starting and Hamilton Products stood to be a major winner in process. For this reason Carol thought the firm's stock price could well increase in the future.

Andre's Decision

Andre decided to buy the convertible bonds. Since his expertise was in painting and not investing, he wanted to get back to his main endeavor as quickly as possible.

Fortunately the stock did well over the next two years increasing in value to $45.50. The bonds also increased in value to $1,250.

It was at this point that Carol called Andre and warned him that a major state investigation into highway construction contracts might be undertaken by a subcommittee of the California legislature. She thought Hamilton Products could be a target of the investigation and suggested that he take his profits and look elsewhere for an investment.

However, Andre was now intrigued by his high returns and decided to hold on to his bonds (somewhat to Carol's disappointment). As it turned out, Hamilton Products was found in violation of state regulations on a number of major contracts and the stock plummeted to $29.75 per share in the next year. During the same time period, a combination of a downgrading of the firm's credit rating and an increase in interest rates caused the yield on straight, non-convertible bonds of those of equal risk and maturity to Hamilton Products to go to 10 percent. Hamilton Product's bonds had 17 years remaining to maturity.

Although Andre was disappointed in the drop in the firm's common stock price, he thought he could take some comfort in the fact that the convertible bonds were an interest paying security, which gave them a basic value below which they normally would not fall.

Required

1. At the time that Andre purchased the bonds, what was the conversion value? What was the conversion premium?
2. When the bonds got up to $1,250, what was the conversion premium?
3. Assume there is a conversion premium of $98 when the common stock price fell to $29.75. What is the price of the convertible bond?
4. What is the pure bond value after interest rates have gone up to 10 percent? You will need to determine the pure bond value based on the annual valuation technique presented in Chapter 10 of the textbook under the "Valuation of Bonds" section. The yield to maturity (required rate of return) is 10 percent and there are 17 years left to maturity. The bonds are continuing to make annual interest payments of 6 ½ percent ($65). The principal payment at maturity is $1,000.
5. How much comfort should Andre take in the pure bond value computed in question 4?

Acme Alarm Systems

Andrew Carter, the CEO of Acme Alarm Systems, could not hide his irritation from Becky Garcia over the proposed buyout of Internet Security, Inc. Becky, a recent graduate from the MBA program at the Darden School at the University of Virginia, knew what was bothering Andrew, and decided to discuss the key issues with him over lunch. She suspected that Andrew was still not use to having a high powered MBA with a six figure salary on his payroll, but the board of directors for Acme Alarm Systems insisted that Andrew hire more young, sophisticated talent to meet the competitive pressures the firm would be facing in the future.

The Proposed Merger

Becky, who was in charge of the firm's mergers and acquisitions development program, had given Andrew a proposal for Acme Alarm Systems to make a buyout offer for Internet Security, Inc. The logic behind Becky's thinking was that Acme Alarm Systems was too tied to the past with its emphasis on home and office alarm systems, and needed to move into the growing area of providing security for documents that were transferred online.

The basic stock market information on the two firms is shown in Figure 1.

Figure 1 Stock Market Data

	Acme Alarm Systems	Internet Security Systems
Total earnings	$50,000,000	$10,000,000
Number of shares outstanding	20,000,000	8,000,000
Earnings per share	$2.50	$1.25
Price-earnings ratio (P/E)	16X	24X
Market price per share	$40	$30

Because Internet Security Inc. was in a more appealing area to investors than Acme Alarm Systems, it had a higher P/E ratio (24x vs. 16x). Also, in order to attract Internet Security as a potential candidate, Becky proposed that Acme make a buyout offer at 40 percent over the stock's current value. Such premiums over market value are common in mergers.

Internet Security Inc. current price	$30
40 percent premium	$12
Proposed offer price	$42

If the offer were made at $42 for the 8,000,000 shares of Internet Security, Inc., the total price would be $336,000,000. Becky suggested offering shares of Acme Alarm Systems to cover the cost and this would require 8,400,000 new shares of Acme stock based on its current price of $40.

$$\text{Number of new Acme Shares} = \frac{\text{Total purchase price of Internet Security}}{\text{Share value of Acme Stock}} = \frac{\$336,400,000}{\$40} = 8,400,000$$

After the merger, Acme would have 28,400,000 shares outstanding (the original 20,000,000 in Figure 1 plus the 8,400,000 shares as part of the merger). The combined earnings of the two firms would be $60,000,000 (based on line 1 of Figure 1). The postmerger earnings per share for Acme Alarm Systems would be $2.11.

$$\frac{\text{Postmerger combined earnings}}{\text{Postmerger Acme shares outstanding}} = \frac{\$60,000,000}{28,400,000} = \$2.11$$

The $2.11 is the number that caught Andrew Carter's attention. When he and Becky arrived at the restaurant for lunch he said, "I can't believe you are recommending a merger which will dilute Acme's earnings per share by $.39 (see Figure 1 for premerger earnings per share of $2.50). He further said, "The analysts on Wall Street will kill us for this decrease in earnings per share."

Required

1. What do you think Becky's response should be?
2. If the merger triggered Acme's P/E ratio to go up by 15 percent, should Andrew be satisfied in terms of the stock price effect?
3. If, in addition to the 15 percent increase in the P/E ratio, total earnings increased by 10 percent because of synergy, should Andrew be satisfied in terms of the stock price effect.

   Recompute earnings per share based on new total earnings and multiply this figure by the new P/E ratio computed in question 2.
4. Assume a 15 percent increase in the P/E ratio and a 10 percent increase in total earnings (as covered in questions 2 and 3), but that Acme paid a premium of 60 percent instead of 40 percent over the market value of Internet Security, Inc. Should Andrew be satisfied in terms of the stock price effect for Acme?

   First, recompute the price per share of Internet Security and the total price that must be paid for its 8 million shares. Then, compute the number of premerger shares that Acme must issue to pay this price. Based on the new total number of shares outstanding, compute postmerger earnings per share (assuming the 10 percent synergy for total earnings).

   Multiply this value by Acme's postmerger P/E ratio (the P/E ratio is up 15 percent as indicated in question 2). The final value will give you the anticipated stock price for Acme. Should Andrew be satisfied with this value?

Security Software, Inc.

Security Software, Inc. (SSI) was a major provider of application software. The firm was proud to be the number two company in the enterprise firewall market.

Firewalls ensure network security for businesses by determining whether to approve or deny access to corporate networks and applications. They have security software that inspects communication from the packet and network layer up to the application layer. SSI's firewall provides integrated access control, authentication, network address translation, content security, auditing, and enterprise policy management solutions. It is based on SSI's Stateful Inspection Technology, which enables the screening of all communication in a highly secure and efficient process.

The Market

In June of 2006, Justin Harper, CEO of SSI, knew the firm would need to go to the financial markets in the next two months to raise new capital. The conversations with his investment banking firm, Southwest Securities, had not been very productive. Carol Travis, a senior vice president of the investment banking firm, had indicated that the market was extremely weak for software providers, but Justin did not realize the extent of the weakness until he examined Figure 1.

Figure 1.   Standard and Poor's Scoreboard on Software Companies

	Index Value	% of S&P 500	Price Changes (%)				
			1 Wk	13 Wks	YTD 2006	2005	5 Yrs.
Information Technology	256.16	14.54	(1.9)	(22.9)	(27.4)	(26.0)	0.8
→Application Software	18.8	0.36	(9.0)	(38.)	(39.4)	(30.9)	(29.3)
Computer Hardware	285.08	3.07	(3.5)	(19.3)	(27.6)	(2.1)	6.0
Computer Storage & Peripherals	207.48	0.30	(3.7)	(30.0)	(38.6)	(74.0)	4.1
Electronic Equipment & Instruments	114.39	0.40	(7.2)	(30.5)	(38.7)	(48.7)	(12.1)
Internet Software & Services	44.79	0.10	0.6	(14.)	(10.0)	(31.2)	NA
IT Consulting & Services	252.34	0.37	(6.7)	(22.2)	(26.1)	5.2	6.6
Networking Equipment	153.92	1.16	(9.1)	(13.7)	(22.0)	(51.4)	7.0
Office Electronics	18.44	0.06	(5.1)	(23.9)	(25.5)	78.6	(31.9)
Semiconductor Equipment	482.03	0.56	(3.9)	(24.4)	(3.5)	7.7	15.7
Semiconductors	319.70	3.08	(3.4)	(31.2)	(28.9)	(16.0)	3.1
Systems Software	442.99	4.09	5.1	(16.1)	(22.2)	5.1	7.9
Telecommunications Equipment	80.85	1.01	(0.7)	(27.2)	(41.3)	(63.3)	(19.3)

His firm fell in the first listed category of "application software." He noted that YTD (year-to-date) firms in that sector had a decline in their stock price of 39.4%, and furthermore it was only mid-June of 2006. Also, in the year 2005, there had been a decline of 30.9%. The only sector in the figure that had performed worse was telecommunications equipment (last line), which was down 41.3% YTD and 63.3% in 2005. That's a cumulative decline over 18 months of 78.46%[1] On average, a telecommunications company that sold for $100 on January, was now selling for $21.54 in June of 2006.

When SSI went public in October of 2002, the stock was initially priced at $22.50. Justin was thrilled that by year-end 2002 it reached $41.75. It hit its all-time high of $71.875 in March of 2004. Currently, the stock was down to $19.50. Justin often woke up in the middle of the night with a sense of disbelief about what happened to SSI's stock and the 50,000 shares he personally owned. He realized he was no longer a millionaire.

---

[1] This number is arrived at by multiplying 100 – 63.3% = 36.7% (the value left after a decline of 63.3% in 2005). The value of 36.7% is then multiplied by 58.7% (the value left after the 41.3% decline YTD in 2006). The answer is 21.54%. This indicates a decline of 78.46% from the initial base of 100.

SSI's Need for Capital

The firm needed to raise $30 million in the financial markets to continue with its program of research and development. R&D was absolutely essential to maintain a position of leadership in the software related firewall industry. Justin indicated that the firm would not be willing to sell additional shares to the public for $19.50 when the initial public offering had been at $22.50 and as recently as March of 2004, the stock had sold at $71.875. Although there had been ups and downs in quarterly earnings due to a weak economy, the company was still as fundamentally sound as the day it went public.

When Justin approached his investment banker Carol Travis with the idea of issuing debt instead of stock, she balked. She explained that similar firms in his industry had bonds that were rated B to Ba by Moody's and BB by Standard and Poor's.[2] This meant they were classified as junk bonds. To be politically correct, most investment bankers call them 'high yield' bonds, but everybody knew what that really meant. Not only did high yield bonds carry high interest rates (2-4% over high quality bonds), but currently there was a very limited market for them, particularly when they were being issued by firms in the computer software industry.

In response to Carol's very lukewarm response to the idea of a bond issue, Justin asked, "Isn't there someway SSI could sweeten up the deal so that bonds might be acceptable for investors."

Carol's Response

Carol responded, "now you are thinking more realistically." While there was no market right now for a debt issue of SSI, if the debt had an option to convert to common stock (while still paying interest), then investors would be interested. Justin quickly snapped back that he was not interested in adding new shares at the current low price of $19.50.

She encouraged Justin to calm down by saying, "One of the advantages of convertible bonds is that they do not have to be convertible at the current market value of common stock. There can be a premium built in the price of the common stock into which the bonds are convertible." Carol went on to suggest a 1,000 par value bond might be convertible into 40 shares of common stock.

Justin was not familiar with the lingo associated with convertibles and asked for a fuller explanation. Carol explained that a conversion ratio of 40 on a $1,000 par value bond meant that the shares were effectively being priced at $25 per share ($1,000 par value/40 conversion ratio). Assuming the bonds had a ten-year life, if and when the bondholders converted in the future, they would be effectively buying the stock at $25 per share.

---

[2] A Ba rating for Moody's is the same as a BB rating by Standard and Poor's.

If the stock, which was currently priced at $19.50, never got up to a market value of $25 over the life of the bond, conversion would not take place. However, if the stock went to over $25, perhaps to $30 or $40, bondholders might have some desire to convert (that is, trade in an initially priced $1,000 par value bond for 40 shares per bond at an effective cost of $25 per share).

Justin liked the concept of potentially getting $25 per share for SSI's currently priced stock of $19.50, but he was not fully sold on the idea. He said, "$25 sounds good based on the terrible hit we have taken in the market, but what if we waited to issue common stock until the stock got back up to $30 or higher, wouldn't we be better off?"

Now it was Carol's turn to snap back. "Justin, it's about time you started being more realistic. You have no assurance that SSI stock is going to go back up to $30 or higher or even $25 for that matter. Besides, you need $30 million right now to remain competitive in the firewall software market. I've already told you that the straight debt market (nonconvertible) is not a viable alternative for SSI. You need a sweetener to attract investors." Justin replied, "Let me have a few days to think this over."

A Second Meeting

When Justin and Carol got back together five days later, he indicated that he had discussed the matter with his chief financial officer and various members of the board of directors and they were amenable to a convertible issue. Carol further fueled his interest by saying, "convertibles normally can be issued at a lower rate than straight bonds."

She went on to say that "although straight bonds likely could not be issued at this point in time, comparable firms to SSI with straight debt already outstanding were paying 11 percent. If similar rated debt (B or Ba) were issued by SSI, but sweetened by the convertibility feature, the rate would probably only be 7.5%." Justin certainly liked this factor and asked if there were any other factors he needed to consider. Carol was quick to answer, "Yes, convertible bonds are potentially dilutive to earnings per share and that is something you will definitely need to consider—but first let's go over some basics."

Required

1. If $30 million of $1,000 par value bonds are issued at 7.5% interest with a conversion ratio of 40:
    a.   How much will the annual interest payments be?
    b.   How many new shares will potentially be created?

2. If Justin raised the $30 million at a current stock price of $19.50, approximately how many new shares would have to be issued? (Round to the nearest whole number.)

3. If he held off until the stock traded at $35, approximately how many new shares would have to be issued? (Round to the nearest whole number.) Is this course of action realistic?

4. By issuing convertibles at 7.5% instead of straight debt at 11%, how much in interest payments will be saved each year?

5. If the convertibles are issued and the price of the stock goes to $35, what is likely to happen to the price of the bonds? Does the convertible bondholder need to convert immediately to take advantage of the increase in the stock price? (Refer to the text if necessary.)

6. If in the future, the corporation wants to force the bondholders to convert, how may it accomplish this? (Refer to the text if necessary.)

7. Carol mentioned that there was potential dilution associated with the convertibles. Assume SSI's condensed balance sheet and income statement, before convertibles were issued, were as follows:

Capital section of the balance sheet

Common stock (10 million shares at $1 par).................... $10 million
Retained earnings ....   50 million
Net worth... $60 million

Income statement

Earnings before interest and taxes..................................... $11,000,000
Interest..   1,000,000
Earnings before taxes   10,000,000
Taxes (30%)..   3,000,000
Earnings after taxes   7,000,000

$$\text{Earnings per share} = \frac{\text{Earnings after taxes}}{\text{Shares of common stock}} = \frac{\$7,000,000}{10,000,000} = \$.70$$

a. Now assume convertibles are issued and the firm is able to increase earnings before interest and taxes by $4,000,000 to $15,000,000 through the investment of the new funds. Based on the new earnings and the interest payments (you computed in question 1), what will the new earnings per share be? For now ignore the additional shares that could be created from the convertibles. You are calculating basic earnings per share similar to that in Table 19-4 of the text.

Fill in below

Earnings before interest and taxes	$15,000,000

Interest ($1,000,000 from the above table plus your answer to question 1 for interest on the Convertibles   _____

Earnings before taxes   _____

Taxes (30%)   _____

Earnings after taxes

$$\text{Basic earnings per share} = \frac{\text{Earnings after taxes}}{\text{Shares of common stock}} = \frac{}{10,000,000} = \underline{\quad\quad}$$

b. Now compute diluted earnings per share as shown in formula 19-2 of the text. You need to add the interest on the convertibles times $(1 -$ the tax rate) to the earnings after taxes that you computed immediately above. This gives you adjusted earnings after taxes.

Then you need to add the number of new shares from the convertibles that you computed in question 1 to the 10,000,000 shares outstanding. The value you get is diluted earnings per share.

$$\text{Diluted earnings per share} \quad \frac{\text{Earnings after taxes} + \text{convertible interest } (1\text{-T})}{10,000,000 + \text{shares created by the convertibles}}$$

8. Comment on the difference between basic and diluted earnings per share. Is the need for computing diluted earnings per share a drawback to the convertibles?

CASE

32

National Brands vs. A-1 Holdings

At 5:30 on Friday afternoon, January 22, 2010. Bill Hall, the chairman and CEO of National Brands, Inc., was clearing up the last of the papers on his desk and looking forward to a relaxing weekend. It had been a good week. The company's annual results were in, and they showed that 2009 had been the best year in the company's history. Sales and net income were up over 8 percent from last year, and there was over $1.1 billion dollars in the cash and equivalents account to invest in the coming year.

The phone rang. It was Maria Ortiz, his secretary. "Did you hear the latest on the newswire?" Maria asked.

"No, what's up?" Bill replied, with a suspicious feeling that his evening wasn't going to be so relaxing after all.

"Kelly O'Brien, head of A-1 Holdings, just announced that he's bought 5 percent of our outstanding shares, and now he's making a tender offer for all the rest at $55."

"I knew it!" Bill spat out. "He was in here just a few weeks ago, talking about whether we would sell the company to him. We turned down his offer because we want to stay independent, and he left after implying we weren't looking out for our stockholders. He's got some plan to restructure the company around a six-member board of directors instead of the 15 we have now. Now he's trying to do it anyway, whether we like it or not!"

"Looks like it," Maria agreed, "so what do you think we should do?" "OK, get ahold of Tom Straw, the chief operating officer, and Doris Faraday in finance, and tell them to get up here for a meeting right away," Bill directed. "Oh, and have Stan Lindner from public relations come, too; we're sure to have a press release about this, and—oh, wait—call my wife, too, and tell her I won't be home until late tonight."

After about half an hour, those that Bill had called began arriving, armed with pencils, papers, and calculators in anticipation of the coming session. Bill, in the meantime, had managed to compile some financial data about A-1 Holdings, which he had summarized on a sheet of paper along with comparable data on his own company, National Brands, (see Figure 1). He passed the sheet around among the others.

"OK, let's start with what we know," Bill led off. "A-1 already has 5 percent of our outstanding shares, and is making a bid for the rest at $55, or 7 1/8 over market."

"I hate to be the devil's advocate," Stan said, thinking of the 1,000 shares he owned personally, "but that sounds like a pretty fair offer. What will happen if he succeeds?"

Most of us will be out of a job, and this company will become just another card in Kelly O'Brien's poker hand," Bill said acidly. "Our employees deserve better than that, so let's talk about what we can do to keep it from happening."

"What about a poison pill?" Tom suggested. "We could take out a fair-sized loan based on our heavy cash position, and A-1 would have a tough time absorbing it—just look at the amount of debt they're carrying now!"

**Figure 1
Selected
Financial Data**

	National Brands	A-1 Holdings
Total earnings expected in the coming year	$ 400,000,000	$ 152,000,000
Number of shares outstanding	113,640,000	61,800,000
Earnings per share	$ 3.52	$ 2.46
Price–earnings ratio	13.6	5.3
Market price	$ 47.88	$ 13.00(rounded)
Book value per share	$ 26.84	$ 6.39
Growth rate before merger	8.53%	19.61%
Liquid assets (cash and equivalent)	$1,153,000,000	$1,736,800,000
Total assets	$5,160,300,000	$2,294,500,000
Total debt	$2,110,300,000	$1,899,500,000
Total equity	$3,050,000,000	$ 395,000,000
Dividend payout ratio	48.0%	0%

"That would probably work, but it's not very good for us, either," Stan agreed. He was still thinking about the seven dollars a share profit to be made in a buyout. "So, how about someone else? You know, a white knight who would top A-1's offer but would keep the structure of the company substantially the same as it is now."

"I don't know who we could ask," Bill said, "and besides that, the basic problem would probably still occur—we would lose our status as an independent entity."

Doris had been working on some figures on her pad, and she spoke up now. "There's another alternative," she said, "that I'm surprised you all haven't mentioned, given the financial status of the two companies."

"What, what!" Bill said. "Don't keep us in suspense!"

"It's the Pac Man defense," she continued, unruffled. "What we do is launch a tender offer of our own for all of A-1's outstanding stock. If it's successful, we not only thwart the takeover attempt but we gain a new business in the bargain."

"Didn't Martin Marietta try that with Bendix back in 1982?" Bill asked. "As I recall, it didn't turn out very well for them."

"You're right, it didn't," Doris agreed, "and no one else has tried it since. But, just comparing numbers here between National and A-1, I think it might work out quite well for us. I've been doing some calculating here, and I think an offer to A-1's shareholders of $17 a share would be accepted, and we could conclude the whole affair rather quickly."

"I'm interested," Bill said. "Tell you what, put your finance staff on it over the weekend and have them work up the proposal formally. Get the legal and accounting people to help you, too. In the meantime, Stan, tip off the news media that we will have an announcement of our own shortly and draft up a public notice for A-1's shares at $17 each. Don't release it yet, but be ready to on Monday. Oh, and be sure to include in it that I said the deal will not cause any dilution of National's earnings per share. One last thing. Doris, draft an open letter to our shareholders for my signature, explaining what's happening and reassuring them that we will keep their company intact and prosperous.

"Any questions? If not, let's get on it—Mr. O'Brien is about to get a surprise!"

Required 1. *a.* A-1 is offering $55 a share for National's stock. How much total cash will it have to raise to buy the company? (The remaining 95 percent?)

   b. Assume A-1 plans to borrow the money needed to make the purchase. If A-1 uses the amount of liquid assets presently on hand at National to offset the amount it needs to borrow, what is the net amount it will have to borrow?

   c. Assuming A-1 does borrow the amount you determined in *b* above, what will A-1's total debt be after the purchase is completed? In making your calculation, consider all forms of debt that the combined firm will have. Now compute A-1's debt-to-equity ratio (A-1's equity will not increase). Given this ratio, do you think it is likely that A-1 will be able to obtain the necessary debt financing?

   d. Suppose instead that A-1 decides to issue stock to raise the money needed for the purchase (i.e., the amount you computed in *b* above will be raised through a stock issue instead of by borrowing). How many shares of A-1 stock will have to be issued? (Assume the price at which it will be issued is $13 and disregard flotation costs.)

   e. If A-1 does raise the money by issuing new shares of its stock, what will A-1's EPS be after the purchase is complete and earnings are combined?

   f. Do you think A-1's shareholders will be happy if this deal goes through? What about the old National shareholders?

Required 2. *a.* If National employs the Pac Man defense and tries to buy A-1 for $17 a share, how much will the total dollar price be?

b. If National wants to finance the purchase by issuing stock, and it plans to use the amount of liquid assets on hand at A-1 to offset the amount of stock that needs to be issued, how many shares if any will have to be issued? (Assume they will be issued at $47.88 and disregard flotation costs.)

c. What will be National's debt-to-equity ratio after the purchase is complete? (Assume it was completed per your calculations in *b* above.) Note National's total equity will not increase since no new shares are issued.

d. Suppose, instead, that National decides to first use A-1's liquid assets to pay down most of A-1's debt. How many shares of National at $47.88 will have to be issued? Use the cost figure from your answer to 2*a*.

e. What will National's new EPS be, assuming the deal is completed per your calculations in *d* above?

f. Is Bill Hall correct in his statement that National's EPS will not be diluted as a result of the purchase of A-1?

3. If National's P/E does not change following the purchase of A-1, what will its stock price be? Is it likely that National's P/E will remain at 13.6? Or do you think it will rise or fall?

4. *a.* Do you think National's Pac Man defense will be successful? Or do you think A-1 will succeed in buying out National?

b. Do you think that National's stockholders are better off as a result of A-1's attack and National's Pac Man defense (assuming it succeeds)?

c. Do you think Kelly O'Brien, head of A-1, should be viewed as a "good guy," whose action will produce more efficient companies, or a "bad guy," who is a destroyer of traditional values and employees' careers?

33

KFC and the Colonel*

Introduction

The story of Kentucky Fried Chicken is the story of Colonel Harland Sanders. The "Colonel," however, was not a real colonel and Sanders was not even a Kentucky native. He was, nevertheless, a prime example of the resiliency of the human spirit because he demonstrated that, even at 66 years of age, after a series of financial fiascoes, it is still not too late to become a business success and a millionaire.

After having lived in obscurity during the first six decades of his life, his benign, bewhiskered countenance became the best-known living advertising symbol throughout the world. Although he was often tough and curt with his employees and associates, he loved children and he donated much of his time and fortune to helping young people. Unpredictable and sometimes erratic in his personal and business dealings, he was unfailingly dedicated to hard work and to the perfection of details. Active until December 1980, when he died at the age of 90, he was a living example of his own philosophy, "A man will rust out faster than he'll wear out:" this was Harland D. Sanders, the kindly curmudgeon who founded Kentucky Fried Chicken.

Harland Sanders was born in Henryville, Indiana, a small town about 17 miles north of Louisville, Kentucky. When he was five or six years old his father died, leaving his mother to raise him and two younger children. What appeared to be a disaster prepared Harland for his future success, because as the oldest child in the family Harland had to take over some of the duties of the household, including some of the cooking. Preparing meals under his mother's direction helped to provide him with the know-how on which he would capitalize many years later. "I cooked just like Mom did, and later when I went into the restaurant business I just kept doing it the same way," he said in an interview in his later years. When Harland was 12, his mother remarried, but his new stepfather did not take kindly to his inherited brood. In fact, on one occasion, he kicked Harland. Hurt by such harsh treatment,

---

* This case was prepared by Robert J. Fitzpatrick, Bellarmine College, Louisville Kentucky.

Harland left Henryville and found a job working on a farm in Greenwood, Indiana. At this time he also attended school, but he dropped out of the seventh grade. He said later that it was the mathematics that did him in.

Job Hopping without Success

Over the next several years Harland led a varied and checkered career, little of which, on the surface, would give any inkling of his later success. In fact, during the early phase of his career he seldom stayed on a job longer than a few months or a year or two at the most. A sketch of his early business experience is fascinating but would hardly qualify for a manual on "How to Become a Millionaire at Age Seventy-Five."

The jobs he held—briefly, in many cases—included collecting fares on a streetcar in New Albany, Indiana; taking care of mules on a cargo boat from New Orleans to Cuba; working as a deckhand on a river boat from St. Louis to Memphis; serving as a blacksmith's helper in Alabama; putting in several years as a railroad yard worker and train fireman, driving spikes and laying rail, and unloading cars at a local mill in Jasper, Indiana.

After the last railroad experience, Harland decided that he had enough of blue-collar jobs and physical work, and he decided to try something less strenuous. He accepted a job with Prudential Insurance Company in Jeffersonville, Indiana, and gave his first evidence as a promoter when he declared that he was "the best insurance salesman in the state of Indiana." He had found his niche, for he reported later that he tore into the job "like a possum after persimmons."

However, he did not remain long with Prudential. He did continue selling, first selling stock for a ferryboat company, then later as executive secretary for the Chamber of Commerce of Columbus, Indiana. Again on the move, Sanders began selling Michelin tires in Kentucky. To promote the sale of his product he wore a "tire suit," made of imitation tires fitting around the body from neck to ankle, the trade symbol of Michelin. His success at attracting the public eye in tire sales may have been the beginning of the idea of the Kentucky Colonel to promote the sale of his famous chicken some years later.

Although he was reasonably successful as a tire salesman, Sanders wanted the opportunity to run his own business, and he persuaded Standard Oil to let him operate a filling station at Nicolasville, Kentucky. Again he displayed his flair for promotion—and perhaps exaggeration. He put up a large sign reading, "FREE AIR," and he later claimed that he was the first filling station operator in Kentucky to wipe off windshields. He also displayed a certain lack of modesty by claiming that "within six months we were pumping more gas than any station in Kentucky." A combination of the depression of the 30's, a decline in farm prices, and drought brought an end to the station in Nicolasville.

Sanders' First Restaurant—Success and Failure

Like the phoenix that rises from the ashes, Harland managed to rise again. He moved to Corbin, Kentucky, and took over a Shell station at a rather desirable location. When he heard one traveler exclaim, "There ain't no decent place to eat around here," he began serving meals in a small room attached to the service station. The station was rechristened "Sanders Shell Station and Café," and, as the food service area was well received and expanded, it was again renamed, "Sanders Café and Shell Station." He hired Nell Ray as a waitress, who was succeeded by her sister Claudia Ledington Price. The latter would become one of his most trusted employees and many years later his second wife. (Sanders' earlier travels and many jobs had brought an end to his first marriage, to Josephine King.)

With the continued success of his restaurant, Harland decided to add a motel, Sanders Motor Court. But cooking was his first love, and chicken was the main item on the menu. The only problem was that frying chicken took about 30 minutes, which he felt was a long time to keep customers waiting. Therefore, he began to experiment with a pressure cooker to cut down on the cooking time, seeking at the same time to keep flavor, moisture, and consistency. Finally, through trial and error, he was able to reduce the cooking time to eight or nine minutes. The significance of the success of this experiment is noted by the fact that one of Colonel Sanders' early pressure cookers is on display at the head office of KFC in Louisville.

In addition to the process using the pressure cooker, however, much of the success of Sanders' chicken was his famous recipe. On one occasion in filling an order for some 500 box lunches, he tried a somewhat different recipe with 11 spices. The food was so well received that he decided to use the recipe regularly. Sanders admitted later that he had used spices that could be found in almost any kitchen and that it was just the proportions that make the difference. He always kept the recipe a secret and even today, according to one reliable report, only two executives at the KFC head office have access to the exact formula.

Sanders' first appearance on the national scene was the recognition he received by Duncan Hines, who had made a stop in Corbin and mentioned the excellent Kentucky fried chicken in his "Adventures in Good Eating." With this added success, Sanders expanded the restaurant to accommodate 142 customers. Later he was offered $165,000 for the restaurant, but he turned down the offer.

Again misfortune struck. In 1955 a new north-south interstate highway (I-75) was routed to bypass Corbin. As a result, Sanders' business dwindled and in 1956 he was forced to sell out for $75,000. After paying off his debts, he found himself scraping bottom. He was 66 years old, drawing about $125 a month in Social Security, and left with very little capital.

Franchising and Success at Last

He still had a form of capital—two, in fact—the famous recipe for fried chicken and a tremendous capacity for work. He had also ventured briefly into franchising. A few years earlier, in 1952, he had sold the rights to his recipe to Leon ("Pete") Harman of Salt Lake City and, at the time that Sanders had been forced to sell his restaurant in Corbin, Harman had some 14 restaurants operating successfully in Salt Lake City, all using the famous recipe with 11 herbs. In effect, the operations in Utah had been a good test market for Sanders' chicken on a broader scale.

With his monetary capital depleted, Sanders realized he could not open another restaurant, but he did realize that with what capital he had, he could try to sell rights or franchises to his special recipe, which had been successful at two locations. So, at age 66, when most men would have retired, Sanders hit the road to sell his then not-so-famous recipe.

In order to make the sale, Sanders would stop at a restaurant, prepare the chicken free, using the special recipe, and then let the owner decide whether he wished to acquire a franchise. The fee was rather modest—four cents per chicken (later increased to five cents). Sanders often tried the chicken himself after preparing it, so he generally got at least one free meal at each stop. Even early in his attempt to sell franchises, Sanders always looked for a quality restaurant—one that would maintain his reputation for a fine product.

Perhaps as the result of the Michelin tire experience, Sanders decided to adopt a new image, that of the Kentucky Colonel. He had actually been appointed a Kentucky Colonel by Governor Rudy Laffon in the early 1930s. The appointments are made rather generously by most governors, and the duties of the colonels include mainly responding to the call to attend the pre-Derby gala dinner and the post-Derby barbecue, with the proceeds going to some charities in Kentucky. No particular uniform is furnished or required. Sanders, therefore, designed his own: a white suit and black string tie. He grew a moustache and goatee, and, since his hair was on the reddish side, he dyed it white to complete the appearance of a "colonel."

Later Sanders was accompanied by Claudia Ledington Price, who had worked for him in Corbin at his restaurant and whom he married in 1949. To add to the "Old Kentucky" touch, she appeared on his business calls wearing an antebellum gown, until finally, when the volume of business had grown, she remained at Sanders' office in Kentucky to manage the paperwork.

By 1960, roughly four years after he had begun selling his franchises actively, Sanders had an estimated 200 outlets under franchise in the United States and half a dozen in Canada—all of this mainly the result of the work of one individual. As the ownership of the company was not publicly held, financial results of Sanders' operations did not have to be made public. It is estimated; however, that Sanders' profits before taxes were in the neighborhood of $100,000 in 1960. By 1963, there were some 600 franchised outlets in the United States and Canada, and annual profits were estimated at $300,000 before taxes.

Enter John Young Brown, Jr.

At this point, Sanders was 73 years of age and still running his company practically single-handedly. Even with his tremendous drive and energy, he may have wondered how long he could continue to operate on his own. Through John Young Brown, Sr., a well-known Kentucky politico, he became acquainted with John Y. Brown, Jr., whom he hired to do some legal work for him. Although a lawyer by profession, John Y., Jr., was actually a super salesman. In order to work his way through the University of Kentucky, he had sold encyclopedias; and by the time he was a senior he was making $25,000 a year. (He would, in fact, go on later to become governor of Kentucky.) When John Y., Jr., discovered that Sanders had no salesmen on the road other than himself, he is said to have remarked, "With my sales background, I began to think what you could do with this business if you had a really aggressive sales program," which perhaps was not giving much credit to the Colonel.

Under the original arrangement between Sanders and Brown, Brown would set up a barbecue business under the unlikely name of Porky Pig's. He would attempt to spin off franchises from the original operation. Brown soon realized, however, that chicken, not pork, was in the pot at the end of the rainbow. Brown felt that the Colonel might be persuaded to part with his creation if he could be convinced that the business would be carried on successfully. In order to make an offer that would be sufficiently attractive to Sanders, however, Brown needed more capital than he personally had available. He, therefore, arranged to get some financial support from Jack Massey, a Nashville millionaire.

Sale of KFC to Brown and Massey

Brown and Massey began discussing the possibility of buying the company from Sanders. The Colonel's first reaction was to snarl, stomp, grumble, and curse. Brown emphasized that, even if the Colonel sold them the company, he would be retained to continue to promote sales and to be its goodwill ambassador. After some further discussion, Sanders—apparently without any fine-line calculations on his part said, "Well, I've been giving it some thought, and I think that two million dollars sounds about right." Brown and Massey at first considered making a counteroffer, but finally decided that, rather than risk losing the deal, they would tell the Colonel that two million also sounded right to them.

Sanders apparently did not talk over the proposed deal with Claudia, who, in effect, had been his closest advisor. She said later that, if she had been consulted, she would have advised against selling at that time. The Colonel also did not consult with the members of his office staff in Shelbyville. Moreover, he had perhaps already come to the conclusion that no one on the staff had sufficient talent to keep the company going without him. That staff had been selected primarily on the basis of nepotism and friendship, rather than on administrative ability. Lee Cummings, the Colonel's nephew, and Harland Adams, his grandson, handled shipments. Several others helped with the office work. Claudia helped to keep the Colonel in touch with problems at the office when he was on the road. However, there was apparently no one with the experience and talent needed to succeed the Colonel in the overall direction of the business.

The Colonel did want to talk with Pete Harman, his original franchisee, before he came to a final decision. All three, Sanders, Brown, and Massey, went out to Salt Lake City to discuss the sale with Harman. The latter indicated the move was a wise one—one that would avoid possible bickering among the Colonel's family and franchisees by offering a continuity of leadership and a firm central control. Following Harman's advice, the Colonel agreed to sign a contract for the sale.

Under the final agreement, dated February 18, 1964, the Colonel was to receive $500,000 by mid-April 1964 and would receive the remaining $1.5 million over a five-year period. In addition, he would be made a director of the company and serve as an ambassador of goodwill and as the principal public relations man. For his services, he was to receive initially a salary of $40,000 a year. Later this would be increased to $75,000 and then to $125,000. Brown and Massey may have had misgivings from time to time about the Colonel's goodwill efforts. Sanders, after having visited certain franchises, was quoted as having said that their gravy "tasted like wallpaper paste." However, whenever Sanders appeared on TV or on the screen in movies, sales jumped.

In the negotiations prior to the final signing of the contract, the Colonel had been offered 10,000 shares of stock as partial payment for KFC, but he declined the offer, commenting in his characteristic and colorful fashion that "stock is just like toilet paper." He also said that "I thought it best to sell [for cash] so that I'd have my estate liquid and I could handle it myself. This way I can do something for my grandchildren and perpetuate the company, too."

The Colonel, however, did not part with the entire company for the 2 million. He retained the rights to the franchises in Canada, where he had formed a separate company. Remembering his early days, he directed that all the profits from this operation should go to aid orphaned boys. He also retained his rights to Florida for his daughter, Margaret. Pete Harman was to retain his rights to Utah and Montana, and the rights to franchises in England were also excluded from the original package.

Following the takeover of the administration from Sanders, Brown assumed the immediate direction of the company, even though Massey had the largest financial interest. Under Brown's aggressive promotion, sales almost doubled and profits more than doubled from 1965 to 1966, as follows:

	Gross Income	Net Income (after-tax)	Earnings Per Share
1965	$8.5 million	$1.5 million	$0.79
1966	$15.0 million	$3.5 million	$1.80

In 1966, following this spectacular showing, Brown and Massey decided to go public and sell stock to outsiders. The share price opened at $15 and soared to $100. In 1968, the stock was split two for one and an offering of a new issue of some 600,000 shares went for $63 per share.

John Y. Brown, Jr.'s, Other Ventures

As successful as he was with Kentucky Fried Chicken, however, John Y. Brown, Jr., was not able to duplicate his efforts in fields other than fried chicken.

There are no Porky Pig's restaurants still in existence. The purchase of H. Salt's Fish and Chips (a British version of fried fish and french fried potatoes) also proved unsuccessful. An attempt to sell roast beef in the KFC outlets also failed. Zantigo's, a try at going Mexican, resulted in the sale of that company to another fast-food firm.

Brown also tried using something closer to Colonel Sanders' formula. He would locate the best hamburger in the country and duplicate it. The result was Ollie's Trolley. Ollie had made what were supposed to be fantastic hamburgers in Florida, and "trolleys" similar to the early food diners were set up throughout Louisville to market the hamburger. The trolley, however, did not work for the most part, as there is only one remaining Ollie's Trolley still operating in Louisville.

Even an attempt to create a chain of Colonel Sanders Inns failed. A prototype was built near the KFC home office in Louisville, but it was sold not too long thereafter to a hotel-motel chain.

Subsequent Sales of KFC to Heublein, Reynolds, and PepsiCo

The success of the Kentucky Fried Chicken business, however, can be measured, at least in part, by the subsequent sales of the business as an entity.

In July 1971, KFC was sold to Heublein, Inc., for a total of $280 million. This was only seven years after the company had been bought from the Colonel for $2 million.

In July 1982, R.J. Reynolds Industries purchased Heublein for $1.3 billion, the purchase made partly in cash and partly in stock of RJR. It is not possible, however, to determine what part of the purchase price applied to KFC, which was included as part of the deal.

In October 1986, R.J. Reynolds did sell KFC as a separate entity to Pepsico for $841 million. At the time, Pete Harman, the second largest franchise holder of KFC, said that they were a kind of family, and "We don't want to be sold again."

All of this may seem to indicate that the Colonel did "do chicken right." His flair for salesmanship and his ability to create an attractive image were important factors in creating a successful business—also his famous recipe and his emphasis on quality. The question that will always remain, however, is: Should he and could he have made a more profitable deal when he sold his company to Brown and Massey?

Required

1. Although a number of business-related items are covered in this case, concentrate your attention on the time in 1964 in which Colonel Sanders sold his business to Brown and Massey. Do you think he acted prudently, based on the information he *currently* had available to him? What additional factors or items should he have considered? You should not be overly influenced by the later success of the business.

Sources used include: *The Colonel* by John Ed Pearce, Doubleday & Co., 1982; *Claudia* by Edward G. Klemm, Jr., Courier-Journal Lithographing Co., 1980; "Kentucky-Fried," by William Whitworth, *New Yorker*, February 14, 1970; *Courier-Journal and Louisville Times*—various articles.